THE DIARY OF ROGER LOWE

OF ASHTON-IN-MAKERFIELD,

LANCASHIRE.

1663 -1678.

*Including a record of burials at Winwick Church
1666-71.*

THE DIARY OF ROGER LOWE

Second edition published by;-

Picks Publishing, 2004
83, Greenfields Crescent,
Ashton-in-Makerfield,
Wigan, WN4 8QY.
Lancashire,
Tel. (01942) 723675.

Printed by;-

Antony Rowe Ltd., Bumper's Farm Industrial Estate, Chippenham,
Wiltshire SN14 6HL
Tel:- (01249) 659705

PREFACE

The original of the interesting Diary, an extract reprint of which fills the following pages, is in the possession of JOHN LEYLAND, Esq., The Grange, Hindley, to whom the editor of the 'Chronicle Scrap Book' has been indebted for the privilege of publishing it in the columns of The Leigh Chronicle devoted to Antiquarian and Historical Notes and Queries. Extracts from the Diary first appeared in the 'Local Gleanings' of The Manchester Courier, but as the Diary is worthy of being published in its entirety, and has, moreover,, great local interest, the whole of ROGER LOWE'S M.S., so far as it can be deciphered, was printed in The Chronicle. Although many of the entries are trivial and valueless, it was deemed better to print all, lest in leaving out something of importance might be omitted, The Diary was therefore for the first time published in extenso in the 'Chronicle Scrap Book'.

Of the writer of the Diary nothing is known beyond what may be gleaned from the facts he himself recorded. He was, at the commencement of his keeping the Diary, an apprentice to a Leigh tradesman, and managed a mercer's shop for his master at the village of Ashton-in Makerfield. The Name of his master can only be conjuncture from a comparison of several entries in the Diary. ROGER LOWE was evidently a young man of pious turn of mind, a sturdy Nonconformist, and somewhat puritanical. He must have possessed pleasing manners to have made for himself, as it is evident from the Diary he did, so large a circle of friends among persons of varied positions in life and adherents not only to his own religious community but to the Churches of England and Rome. His associations with the ejected Nonconformist ministers were frequent, and with the local clergy of the Established Church he was also on terms of friendship. He mixed freely in the amusements of his neighbours; and, being a 'scholar', was the confident of their private affairs, made their wills, drew bonds for them, assisted the village constable in his writings, was in great request as a reporter of the sermons, and undertook, when his friends needed the aid of a ready pen, the delicate task of inditing love letters wooing by proxy. The local entries in the Diary give a lively picture of everyday life in a Lancashire village and the country round during the reign of Charles II., written at the time by an observant young man, living a somewhat active life an brought into daily intercourse with his neighbours and friends in Ashton, Leigh, Newton, Winwick and other villages in South Lancashire. It is, however, somewhat remarkable that no political references are met with in the Dairy, and for what it tells the stirring national events of the Commonwealth and the reign of Charles II. might never have occurred. Much light is, however, thrown upon many points in local antiquarian matters, some of which are marked by the Editorial Notes in the reprint.

The Diary itself is contained in a small quarto book about 150 pages, very closely written, and, as might be expected from it's age, in some place almost illegible. Mr. LEYLAND, in whose families it had been for many years, has had the original transcribed, and from the transcript the reprint has been made, some manifest blunders and errors being corrected by comparison with the original. At the end of the Diary is a lengthy Obituary, which contains much valuable information, especially as the existing registers of the Chapelry of Ashton do not commence till after the date of the Diary - the baptisms commencing in 1698, the Marriages in 1712, and the Burials not being recorded in the Church Books till 1764. The complete reprint of this portion of the Diary is therefore of value to local genealogists.

It should be understood that the reprint is from the newspaper type, as it appeared week by week in the Chronicle during the autumn of 1876. It is published in a collected form for the use of Lancashire antiquarians, as more convenient for preservation and reference than newspaper slips. No pretence is made of editorial work; and an acknowledgement is due for some of the explanatory notes to the Editor of the 'Local Gleanings' of 'The Manchester Courier' and his contributors. In issuing ROGER LOWE'S Diary in this form the Editor of The Leigh Chronicle simply desire to add what little he can to the stores of the County History, and to place before the antiquarian students of Lancashire some matter for examination to which they have not hitherto had the opportunity for conveniently referring.

J.R.

'Chronicle' Office, April, 1877.

Note. - The entry in the Diary for November 3, 1664, is incorrect. The Diarist evidently uses the word 'wassail' in its proper sense.

The Editor of The Leigh Chronicle.

ROGER LOWE

Roger Lowe may fairly be called a Lancashire Pepys. He began his diary in 1663, three years after Pepys started his, and, although the Lowe Diary, except for a few fragments at the end, covers but three years, some of the vitality and comprehensiveness that characterised the record of the admiralty clerk had crept into the jottings of the apprentice shopkeeper. The men he had to do with were villagers, traders, rural preachers, farmers and farm labourers; the young women he met and kissed were farmers' daughters, innkeepers' daughters and servants, lively north country lasses who knew their own minds. Instead of the gay city and grandeur that Pepys described, Roger wrote of a village and of the country adjacent, where he took part in whatever gaiety there was, and helped to make it.

The village was Ashton in south Lancashire, now known as Ashton-in-Makerfield, not far from Leigh, Warrington and Wigan, and only a day's journey on horseback from the growing centres of Manchester and Liverpool. It was there that he was serving a nine years' apprenticeship, keeping a small general shop for his master, Thomas Hamond, who lived in Leigh.

Keeping shop was a task that meant constant worry for Roger and imposed much attention to detail. The commodities that his master sent from Leigh were duly charged to his account; other commodities he bought from farmers, from shopkeepers in larger towns, from cloth men, and at fairs. At times he was busy making brief expeditions and driving bargains to replenish his house supply of wax, honey and candles, or to purchase a quantity of hour glasses or scythe stones. besides keeping the shop stocked, he had to collect sums from customers, who had been trusted for their purchases and that was a task which took him on many a long walk. The shop weighed most heavily on Roger's mind in the days preceding the time when he expected the master would come or send to have the accounts cast up. What his master might have to say about the state of the business would worry him so much that he often unable to rest at night. But the master seems to have been content to find the accounts straight. At intervals Roger could show profits of £13, £21 and £18. How he made such profits is hard to understand, for the margin between buying prices and selling prices does not appear to have been large, and a number of customers who were worse than slow in making payment, was considerable. For his favourable balances Roger's reward was usually a new suit. Once the customary gift was reduced to a coat which Roger aggrievedly refused to accept. On the whole the master seems to have been kindly disposed to his apprentice but only decorously generous. The master's wife, always called 'my Dame' by Roger, was friendly to the Ashton youth and sometimes made up for her husband's caution.

If the rewards of the shop for the apprentice were not great, the work was not particularly arduous. It was the success of the enterprise not the labour it entailed that tormented Roger. He tended the shop himself, and whenever he went on errands business had to be suspended. Whoever needed to buy could - and did - send word round the village for him to return. If he were at some distance, he would learn from the villagers on coming back, what customers had been inquiring for him.

It was not only buying commodities and collecting debts that took him away from the shop. His place was necessarily a kind of village centre, and it behoved him to be a good fellow. That meant frequent trips to the alehouse where he had to take his turn at paying for the drinks, and this was no small expense to an apprentice. Nearly every day he entered soberly in his diary the amount of this tax on merriment, or once in a while noted with satisfaction that he did not have to pay. He bestowed his patronage as well as he knew how upon all the alehouses in the vicinity, and he was not one to shirk his duty that way. 'Came to Goose Green', he wrote, 'and there stayed in a alehouse; but it was my great trouble to stay or to have gone to this gait, only they were good customers to me and I durst not but go for fear of displeasure.' He felt obliged to stop at Gawther Taylor's tavern, for Taylor's wife bought goods at his shop. 'She said if I would not come, then farewell'. When Mr. Wood, the minister, came to his shop and reprimanded him for being too much in ale, he excused himself that he could not trade if sometimes he did not spent two pence. So persistent was the call of good companions that there were days when Roger was but little on duty. One afternoon he bowled for hours, then rushed back to shut the shop, and returned to finish the game. When he did stay in the shop all day it was a fact worthy of note in the diary.

Roger was more than a shopkeeper to the community. He was accountant, solicitor, scrivener and errand boy in general. When two men quarrelled over their trading, Roger was called in to go over the figures or to arbitrate the issue. Sometimes he drew up indentures. People looking for houses would ask Roger to accompany them and help them with the details of their leases. Occasionally he was summoned to write a will and, as he himself put it, he could do that somewhat handsomely. A villager such a Thomas Heyes might feel equal to composing his own documents, but he would have Roger in to read over the writings. One man wished his son taught how to write and reckon, and Roger good-naturedly tried his hand as educator. He wrote letters for a large and mixed clientele, business letters to London or nearby towns, letters from wives to husbands, even love-letters. When John Hasleden confessed his infatuation for a wench in Ireland, it was Roger who penned a love-letter from him. He even obliged Anne Barrow, an old flame of his, when she wished to answer a love-letter from Richard Naylor, and Richard acknowledged the favour by sending him a lemon. Clients were, however, were not always so well satisfied with the outcome of Roger's letters. Ellin Ashton complained that Roger had written to her son matters which she had not instructed him to put in. 'A false lie'. Roger declared to his diary, but he hurried off next day to spend two pence at Ellin's and conclude peace. Roger's pen was also at the disapproval of local ministers who indicted verses on death of a village lass or gave him a long recipe for a purer life: potions composed of a quart of repentance, nine handfuls of faith, and a quantity of other metaphysical ingredients.

Writing was Roger's principle avocation, but his usefulness did not stop there. Anyone with an odd job was sure to think first of Roger, because he was both accessible and willing. When a gentleman needed a men to go to Lancaster and then to London, what was more natural than to ask Roger to find some dependable person? He got track of a maid for Anne Greinsworth, whose accounts he was always going over, and those letters he wrote to her brother in London. Thomas Johnson of Liverpool sent a lad into the neighbourhood on a business errand and instructed him to report to Roger, who was to accompany him and supervise the transaction. The schoolmaster at Ashton heard of a teaching vacancy near Preston and solicited Roger's help in approaching the right people. In more delicate matters his services were welcomed. He could say prayers at the birth of a child. At the bedside of William Hasleden's wife, he sat reading The Practice of Piety until 'she gave up the ghost'. No one in the neighbourhood was more popular as a mourner at funerals. Unusually he went of his own accord, but often he was specially sent for. Sometimes he was asked to bid the guests, sometimes to sit in the cellar and tell off the drawing of flagons.

Next day there were more errands for the living. John Jenkins must have his help to prick out sheaves of barley; John Hasleden wanted his company to hunt up a workmen; John Potter, on his way to have a tooth pulled, needed Roger with him to supply courage. Or very likely the local officials thought it would be wise to have Roger along when they were about some of their duties. The constables were glad of his help when they collected the poll tax. One night he went round with one of them to make private search at every alehouse. When money was gathered for the poor of London after the Great Fire, Roger was one of those who went about soliciting the contributions. The constables of neighbouring villages came to him to write out their presentiments for the assizes. 'When I had done, I writ: "Poor is provided, highways repaired, these queries answered, and clerk unrewarded," ' The constables laughed heartily, but it is not recorded if they took the hint.

For such services, it is hard to say how much he was paid. Widow Low gave him a shilling for copying a sermon; and old Jenkins paid him eleven shillings and sixpence for making a will and preparing other legal papers. In one instance he was given sixpence for a bond, and by nightfall the alehouse keeper had it. In general he received fees for drawing up formal documents and for making accounts. Apparently he could do as he pleased with such income, thorough once his master would not let him keep the three pounds accumulated by writing. In the case of many services Roger would have little need to report his revenue. Custom prescribed no specific remuneration. Services were performed out of good nature for persons who could not or would not offer money compensation. These thrifty Lancashire folk were likely to reward him with a drink at the alehouse or to assume that their patronage bound him in return to do miscellaneous services for them. Favours circulated as much as money.

Roger's willingness to help everyone meant that he had a wide circle of acquaintances and friends, ranging from labourers and farmers, innkeepers, apothecaries and shopkeepers to Nonconformist ministers and parsons. His social boundaries can be approximately determined by the fact that he deemed it a signal courtesy to be invited to call upon Robert Greinsworth, under-sheriff of Lancashire and son of that Anne Greinsworth whose accounts he looked after. At the same time he was 'comely entertained' by Anne Greinsworth herself. He was pleased and more comfortable when he spent an evening with the village schoolmaster or with old Mr. Wood, who had been the parson and was now a Nonconformist minister.

With the minister he would chat about 'ministers and other things', about the sufferings of Mr. Calamy, Mr. Gee and other famous Nonconformist divines. At the alehouse, too, there might be talk of religion, but the conversation was likely to be more personal, 'about trading and how to get wives'. Talk about the affairs and griefs of 'our calling' would be carried forth from the inn and finished late at night in Town Fields. Roger had many of his troubles to tell and had the gift of listening at length to the troubles of his friends. With old Peter Leland he walked into a field called Horsehead-under-Bank where Peter gossiped on about his woes - a daughter had the falling sickness, one son was void of a calling, the other weak and infirm - until both Roger and the old man fell asleep in the field.

He was dependent upon his friends and their loyalty, he could share their moods of depression and offer sympathy, he was with them in merriment. If they never quite dispelled the feeling that he was alone in the world, they furnished nevertheless a kind of protection against moods of fear and despondency. When he had a tiff with any of them he was in anguish until he could patch up the difference.

He had friends of every age, but his cronies were those of his own generation. With John Hasleden, Thomas Smith, Roger and James Naylor, and John Potter, he passed many an evening in the tavern, lending a hand if one of them from ill tippling began to wind his way home. Roger would sum up such gatherings by the comment: "We were very merry."

For his circle of young men a really happy evening included the village belles. And it is recorded that the young men visited the maidens where they lived and worked, and walked with them in the fields and lanes. On these strolls it seems that often the young people craved the assistance of a third party, and there was no Cupid's proctor better qualified or more called upon than Roger. He would coax the girl to meet the young man, or go with the man to visit the girl, he would remain in attendance at the courtship, and help to carry on negotiations.

He had almost as many friends among the married folk. Sarah Hasleden would lead him off to supper and give him roast goose, and other wives would lure him to a meal or to the alehouse. He was always being asked the husbands to come and spend the night. Any woman who was getting up an 'ale' with music and other inducements expected Roger's presence.

Friendship gave entree to all the village cheer. It is true that the inhabitants had no theatres, no bull-fights or bear-baiting near at hand, no Vauxhall, none of the countless diversions that Pepys' London furnished, no tailored amusements. Rather there was ready-made fun altogether dependent on the society of one another and upon the stimulus that the tavern afforded. Weddings, christenings, the end of an apprenticeship, the departures or return of a villager, were public events; even funerals were turned into occasions. A deceased native was mourned respectfully enough, but the preparations for the funeral took place amidst a buzz that betrayed the eagerness of the young men and women to have a day free from shopkeeping or brewing, from planting or cleaning pans. Messages flew back and forth while the expectant mourners made plans for the horses for each maid, it would seem, must have a man, preferably a young man, to ride before her. The mourners crowded the house and overflowed into the yard and the chambers overhead, so that no one noticed particularly if the young people were tying up the loose ends of their courtships while waiting for the procession to start. Death, remarked Nicholas Breton is the mourner's merry day.

The funeral became the occasion when the customary food and wine was served. Failure to respect that custom curtailed the attendance of guests after the burial of the corpse. At Ann Johnson's funeral the mourners were offered only a loaf, where at Roger, hungry and angry, fled to Wigan for refreshment. To the funeral of Anne Taylor, Roger went fasting, not without anticipation. 'At noon when we had buried the corpse and expected according to custom to have some refreshment, and were a company of neighbours sat together round about a table .... the Doctor comes and prohibits the filling of any drink till after prayers.' Roger debated unhappy. 'At last with much vexation I gat to Ashton with a hungry belly, and Honest Thomas Harrison and right true hearted Ellin, the hasty, yet all love, did much refresh my hungry pallet with a big cup once full and after that half full again of good pottage.'

Weddings were not hampered by the proprieties, but Roger seldom described them with gusto he bestowed upon funerals. He was the best man at John Hasleden's wedding, and attended that of his friend, Thomas Smith. There was celebration when his fellow apprentice, John Chaddock of Leigh, was married. After the ceremony Roger was dispatched to Wigan to buy seven yards of ribbon. ' Were each of us had a yard of ribbon of 12d. per yard, and so rid through town.' It will be remembered that when Leonard Wheatcroft was wed, the ribbons were the prizes for the winners of the race to Ashover.

It must not be supposed that Roger and his friends had to wait on marriage for their gaiety. An old Ashton friend who had moved away to York sent a shilling to be spent by his former alehouse mates, and Roger drank his share. Sunday was likely to be a convivial day; Roger would go from one house to another, getting food here and drinks there. On a December Sunday John Potter and he went into an alehouse and found it so thronged that they could not sit by the fire. 'We sacrificed ourselves o'er the two penny flagon in a cold chamber.'

These good Nonconformists do not seen to have been different from others in their pleasures or sports. They fished, they pursued rabbits and hedgehogs, and occasionally foumarts (polecats.). Now and then there was a horse race. Roger bowled rather often, and to his loss. One time he stopped to look at a great company gathered on the heath 'with two drums amongst them.' The young men were playing prison bars and Roger with a scoffing air towards what he had learned to do concluded that it was but a vanity. He must have been more diverted at Chorley fair when he saw a play, the subject of which was the life of a man from his infancy to his old age. But as for singing, that indispensable accompaniment of jollity, there is no evidence that roger and his friends sang anything butt psalms. by the rousing rendition of a psalm at the roadside Roger could transform a sad mood into a hearty one. Yet though his own singing had a purpose, he enjoyed music too; at Manchester he entered the church just as the choristers came in, and was 'exceedingly taken with the melody.'

It was a fondness for music, but it was the novelty as well, that made him hasten to Mr. Barker's to see the new organ, something he had never heard before. He had eyes in his head that looked out for what might be seen, whether it was coal pits, a burning well, or an acquaintance in the stocks. At Ormskirk he made it a point to enter the church and gaze on the tomb of the Earl of Derby. when at Chester fair he went into the castle to see a man condemned to die. 'A pretty young man he was, and very sorry I was.'

It is interesting to find this seventeenth century apprentice displaying towards old ruins some of the melancholy interest characteristic of the Horace Walpoles and the John Byngs of the next century. He thought it a pity, when he viewed Bradley Hall, to see 'so goodly a fabric lying waste.' He was impressed with the country seat still in habitation. A female servant ushered him through the place. 'We looked up and down, stood upon a hill and saw the land round about. It's the pleasantest place that ere I saw, a most gallant prospect. Came to Ashurst Hall and Elizabeth took us into the chambers up and down - a most pleasant place and gallant walks.' Seldom before the eighteenth century did people stop to admire the view. Before that time country houses were nearly always on low ground, near water, and away from wind and storm, where there was no prospect of any kind. Indeed where there was a prospect, the front of the house sometimes turned its back on it. 'The houses of the gentry,' wrote Thomas Fuller, 'are built rather to be lived in that to be looked on, very low in their situation, for warmth and other conveniences.' Roger had been to the residences of the gentry on business, but to be shown through such a house seems to have been an experience. His curiosity was indicative; there was a breadth about it; he was a peasant but a good deal more.

He had certain advantages over his class. Keeping shop gave him a wide acquaintance with people; it enabled him to mingle comfortably even in circles where his master, for instance, did not appear. Moreover, his education and his utilitarian knowledge gave him an authority that came just short of elevating his position. He was something of a local character.

His own personality contributed to the effect. We cannot but observe that the people of Ashton seldom omitted to pick Roger up on the way to the alehouse, that a man or woman who intended to travel on foot or on horse to a nearby village always invited Roger to come along, that ministers on their way through the district made a point of dropping into Roger's shop and invariably sent for him, if they happened to be anywhere nearby. It was not merely that he was of an oncoming disposition and had that liking for his fellows which ensured their appreciation of him. He was more worth listening to than any of his neighbours. He had a way with him, and the community recognised as much.

His gift of expression and his humorous way of talking appears throughout the diary, and appears at its perfection in two stories he told about himself. It would be hard in the literature of the seventeenth century to find a better peasant humour than is to be seen in those narratives. In each of the stories he dramatised himself as a comic character. He was once leading a ram by a rope towards Leigh when the tup butted him. 'I, being unacquainted how to act with tup in rope let him have the length of rope, and tup ran always backwards and fell on me, so that I was put in a terrible fright what to so to save my shins ... I laid me down with my head upon my legs, thinking to save my legs, and he gave me such a pat on the head made me turn up white eyes. I thought and was half afraid lest I gotten old Nick on the rope. I prayed to God to deliver me from the tup and rope, but in conclusion my bones were sore, brains sick, and heart dead with fear what to do with tup. I looked at tup with an angry countenance but could not tell how to be revenged. Kill him I durst not ... Fair words would not pacify him nor angry countenance affright him; but at last I resolve upon a manly resolution thus : "What, Hodge, art in a strait? What's the reason for this fear and grief? A tup. Does that daunt thee? Stand upon they legs and fight manfully in answer thereunto." I did, and gat a kibbow out of the hedge, and tup and I fell to it, but the tup o'er came me. I could do no good, but down on my knees again. I get hold of tup's horns and on one of his feet and cast him. "So now, tup, I intend to be revenged on thee," and smote him on the head. But with great difficulty I gat him to Leigh, but I never was in such a puzzle in all my life as I was with that tup.' Here Roger, by way of finale, reviewed once more his tussle with the tup and concluded: 'But since I have known tups, the very name of tups hath been trouble to me ears.'

Roger went on with his second story, 'that the world may see straits I have been in and what troubles I have undergone in my life'. When Roger lived with Mr. Livesey he was sent to Mr. Henry Lee of High Leigh about a minister for the chapel. Arriving at dinner-time very hungry he was set at table with servants. 'Every servant a great bowl full if podige [pottage], upon a great trencher like a pot lid I and all others had, with a great quantity of podige. The dishes else were but small and few. I put bread into my podige, thinking to have a spoon, but none came. While I was thus in expectation of that I could not obtain, every, and having a horn spoon in their pockets, having done their podige, fell to other dishes. Thought I, these hungry Amelikites that I am almost gotten amongst will devour all if I do not set upon a resolution ... I cast an eye to my trencher - there was whole sea of podige before ... Well, I resolved: "Hodge, if thou will have any victuals here thou art fallen into, what a hungry spirit possesses these men. Thou must now resolve upon action." And a speedy dispatch with these pottage accordingly I did, and sweeped them as if I would have drunk. Then when I had them in my mouth I was in such a hot fire in my mouth turned meditation into action, but at last, to my lamentation, I was worse than before. I would gladly have given 5s. that I had but had the benefit of air or a northern blast ... Help myself I could not for the table was before me and a wall behind me upon my back, a woman with her falsket upon right hand, And a man with his codpiece upon the other, and in this sad condition I sat bothering, knew not what to do best. Those few pottage I tasted was both dinner an supper. I at last rise form table with a hungry belly but a lamenting heart, and e're since I have been cautious how to sup pottage, and likewise wary. Nothing worser to a man than over-hastiness, especially in hot concernments; hot women, hot pottage, and angry tups beware of and pray to be delivered from.'

It is hardly surprising that the injunction against women leapt to Roger's tongue as he wound up the story, for when Roger had trouble with his friends, often as not, it arose out of his own or his companions' love affairs. Those affairs are in some ways the most significant matters in the diary. Among the gentry in the seventeenth century - we know more of them because their letters were often kept - fathers and mothers had most to do with the making of matches. In that class money was certainly the pivot of the projected felicity. It was hardly the same with the common folk of Lancashire. Parental approval was not indeed to be scoffed at, as Roger found out, nor a comfortable income to be despised, but the actual courting was left in the hands of the young people themselves. Nor was it a masculine affair. The young women did their full share, and in hearty peasant fashion made their preferences apparent. 'At night', wrote Roger, 'I met with Margaret Wright, Mr. Sorowecold's maid. She needs would have me with her home. I went and she made much for me.' Not every young woman, nor every young man for that matter, was as direct as Margaret. Anne Hasleden resorted to the method of inviting a friend to assist her, sundry times asking Roger to bring Henry Lowe to call.' Henry proved entirely willing, and when he and Roger kept their appointment with Anne, they were served spiced drinks and 'very much made of we were'. Making much of a young man was apparently an informality that Lancashire lasses understood and the young men appreciated.

The informality must have gone too far sometimes, but we have only one instance of that recorded by Roger. 'I was entreated per Richard Asmull to go with him and John Hasleden into Hindley. There was a wench had laid a child on him. So we went, and in Mr. Lanckton['s] fields she was, and she ardently manifested him to be the father of the child in her womb, so we parted.' Asmull then took Roger and Hasleden into the alehouse and spent sixpence on them and Roger went on his way without comment or any indication that his puritan soul was shocked.

The reliance that Roger's friends placed upon him in their love affairs did not signify that he was wise in his own. He was popular enough with the young women, his attentions were often welcomed and even sought; he was in his way even a favourite with them. But although he was determined to have a bride, and was obviously more eager than particular, the young women of Ashton and its environs received his proposals with unfeigned reluctance. His tendency to be on with a new love before he was off with the old, was not unnoticed. He was once discoursing in the alehouse with Roger Naylor about Aesop's fable of the dog who caught at the shadow and lost the subspace, whereupon Naylor applied the lesson to Roger suggesting that Roger might be doing just that. Roger was amazed and hurt. The girls of the community had long since ceased to be amazed, and they were naturally not convinced by Roger's professions of love. He had another disadvantage in their eyes. So far as they could judge, his instability in flirtations was more than matched by the inadequacy of his prospects.

Roger had innumerable encounters, but he elaborated on two affairs that wrung from him expression symptomatic of passion in any age or clime, one with Mary Naylor and the other with Emm Potter. When the diary opens he had been wooing Anne Barrow, but had grown tired of her, 'fearing the acceptance of love,' He made it plain to Anne that his attentions were over, a painful business for one of his wooing disposition. a few months later he was instrumental in furthering James Naylor's courtship of her.

Almost at once after his dismissal of Anne, he fell into a tempestuous affair with Mary Naylor, vows of eternal love alternating with quarrels, tears and reconciliations. The two resolves 'because we lived severally that we would not act so publicly as others, that we might live privately and love firmly, that we might be faithful to each other in our love till the end'. And Roger marked this occasion as the first night he had stayed up a-wooing in his life. But Mary's mind was vacillating. 'I went to Roger Naylor ['s], and Mary cried to me, said she would have nothing to do with me. was highly displeased at me; but in the conclusion she was well pleased, would have me to go with her day after to Bamfurlong, and she would go before, and to signify she was before, she would in such a place ay a bough in the was, which accordingly she did, and I found it'. It was love in the country lanes, but not quite the sweet romance or fated hopelessness of which the poets tell. Yet Roger knew how to use the lanes to his advantage. If he found Mary moody, he would follow her down the lane while 'she went give calf a drink', and she would change her manner. Next day she would drop in at the shop, be all friendliness, and put the rhetorical question, 'Am not I a wise wench to engage myself thus?' But matters ran for from smoothly. Mary's father did not approve of Roger, and Mary became frightened lest her friends could cease to respect her.

Even in his darker moments Roger believed that the Lord was attending to the matter in his own way, for one day, after talking to Mary, he wrote: 'When I came home there was a direct N and half M providentially made upon my breeches, plain to view in any man's sight, made of mire with leaping.' It was and looking after that he was able to find Mary alone and very pleasant; that evening he went back to his shop, lit a candle, and jubilantly sang the seventy-first psalm.

But Mary remained afraid of parental displeasure. Roger would look her out when her father went to chapel on Sunday or left his house on another day, and would visit her; she would come to the shop and he would take her part way him.

Mary's fluctuations furnished no solid mooring for Roger's own inconstant nature. He was the sort of person who would not wait too long on her or on Providence. His sorrows when Mary had frowned on him and refused an explanation had not restrained him from presenting his service to Ellin Marsh, who had a house and a living. This he did by a private mediator. Emm promised to meet him of he would keep the conference secret, and that at the same moment, Roger was old too glad to do.

One might have supposed that an eternal friendship with Mary Naylor and secret negotiations with Ellin Marsh would have been all that Roger could manage with impunity. On the contrary he was capable, without a pang, of renewing his old friendship with Anne Barrow at the moment when he was persuading Anne to look with favour upon his friend James Naylor. He entreated Anne for himself 'to be the next in succession if in the case they two should break off, to which she did not say no, neither yes'. It was Anne whom Roger had shaken off a few months before. She might well hesitate to fish for this amorous eel a second time.

At the same time he continued to court Mary. Her love for him he believed lightened his griefs. Like others he could find sweet love remembered an anodyne for his outcast state. He was certain that his affections were centred upon Mary's virtues and womanly qualities, but we may suspect that he was in that stage of young man's development when he loved the emotion rather than the person who induced it.

Roger had by no means finished fitting extra strings to Cupid's bow. In the very midst of these complicated affairs he wrote: 'I was at this time in a very fair way for pleasing my carnal self, for I knew myself acceptable with Emm Potter, notwithstanding my love was entire to Mary Naylor in respect of my vow to her, and I was in hopes that her father countenanced me in the thing.' He saw nothing out of the way in his behaviour, but he was presently shocked to the core at the duplicity of others. It was James Naylor who blasted Roger out of this particular intrigue. James, who must have come to the suspect that his advocate was putting in a few words for himself with Anne Barrow, rifled his sister's band-box, purloined all the letters that Roger had written her, and let Anne read the letter's secrets with Mary. Then indeed did Roger's faith in human integrity all but collapse. His 'pretended friend' he dubbed a 'stinking rascal, a 'malicious, dissembling, knavish rascal'. He concluded that if people could do things like this only God could be trusted, but on the way home John Damme gave him some apples, which were immediate comfort.

Roger took this episode hard. He babbled about the vale of death and his need of God's rod and staff to comfort him. He never did regain the confidence of Anne Barrow and Mary Naylor. Anne, like a sensible girl, eventually took Roger aside for a calm rectifying of all business between them, and he discreetly withdrew. So for Mary Naylor, he was nearly at the end of his eternal friendship with her. She is not mentioned in the diary for months, but when Roger finally saw her again, although she received him affectionately, he told her she was a false dissembling person, 'She took it heinously', Roger observed, not without satisfaction. Shortly after Roger tried to patch things up. Mary was kindly but refused to renew the old relationship. 'I set her light as she did to me, and so parted.'

ix

Meanwhile Roger had not overlooked his prospects with Emm Potter. A month after his parting with Mary, Emm came to comfort him through a day's illness. His affair with her began to take on the intensity of the recent one with Mary. He resented another's attention to Emm, although the admiration of another man may have stimulated his determination to win her. As other girls had done, Emm paused on the brink of serious alliance with Roger, and he was in consequence in a sad fit, utterly disconsolate again. He took his troubles to one of Emm's friends and wept so freely that she pitied his state and arranged for him to meet Emm, with the happy result that they 'professed each other['s] loves to each other.' It was next evening, after attending prayers, that Roger made his way to the window of the chamber where Emm lay, and 'would gladly have come in'. But Emm was a wise wench. 'She durst not let me in, but she rise up to the window, and we kissed.'

The preliminaries thus attended to, the affair went on for months, as it had with Mary. Roger and Emm quarrelled and made up, etc. And as usual Roger had his mind on other possibilities; he heard of a desirable wife in Chester worth £120 and jumped at the idea. 'I was glad of the business and had some hopes of freedom from my master.' But nothing came of this proposal, and Roger continued his interest in Emm.

That such a periodically lovesick boy should be extraordinarily religious is not surprising. It was at religious services that he felt perhaps most happy. The reader will remember that in the reign of Charles II all religious services save those of the Established Church were forbidden by law. Roger was Nonconformist, and Nonconformists had to hold their meetings as quietly as possible. At one meeting we see the minister whispering to the worshippers the time and place of the next coming together, which was likely to be on a Sunday, but might well be during the week, and usually at a private house. Once when Roger's friends were gathered in a house for a service, a few Papist women came in unexpectedly, and the meeting had to be called off. This secrecy no doubt spiced the worship and gave an adherent like Roger a sense of importance. Unobtrusive meetings were held in Ashton, when the diary opens, under the ministry of Mr. Woods, who had between the curate there before the puritan ministers in 1662 were put out of their pulpits. To the regret of his followers, Wood moved to Cheshire, and for months after his departure there was a dearth of local services. Roger was forced to travel to neighbouring villages that he might hear a sermon, an inconvenience mitigated by halts at alehouses with friends on the way to and from the services. Mr. Wood, however, made periodic trips back to Ashton to revive his flagging flock.

In this flock Roger had a definite position. He was the mainstay of Mr. Wood and of the other ministers; at the services John Robinson's and at other houses he was an easy figure. If for any reason the minister was absent, Roger could repeat a sermon to the assembled faithful; he did equally well to a Sunday gathering of young people in the fields. At services he might feel exercised to pray, but it is noticeable that when he did not feel so disposed, he would refuse. Whatever his position as a shopkeeping apprentice, his place in Nonconformist activities must have given him a confidence in himself that he often needed. When he wrote, after an evening at Robinson's,. 'Oh how comfortable is the communion of the saints', we may suspect that his heart was warmed not only by a spiritual glow, but by the realisation of the esteem he commanded in his religious circle.

That esteem was doubtless justified by his knowledge of theology and by his ability to carry on an argument about it. Theology was his intellectual outlet; there was nothing he liked better to discuss, even though the discussion often tended to become acrimonious. He was glad when he could report that in the disputations he and his friends had been 'very loving', but that was far from the usual case. When he argued with a friend about the claim of Presbytery versus Episcopacy, the two men were so stirred up against one another that they did not speak for two or three days. With the vicar of Huyton Roger threshed out the question of the Anglican orders. 'He said they were apostoical. "Yea," quoth I. "they are apostatical from the truths of God".' Roger was afraid that the vicar was displeased, but on a later visit to Huyton, he and the vicar enjoyed a merry time together at the alehouse. Roger contended with Catholics as well, defending Luther against jibes of a papist friend; but there is nothing to indicate that he had the horror of Romansism common amongst puritans. He was too interested in theology not to listen to anyone might have to say about it. In his diary he relates that, hoping to get his mind off Emm Potter, he went several times to hear the Bishop preach, and doubtless approved of his sermon 'against atheisticalness.'

Listen and argue Roger might, but he did not intend to be browbeaten. Because he had not stood at the reading of the gospel, he received what determined 'some piece of disgrace' from Mr. Atkinson, the clergyman who rook charge at Ashton in 1668. After evening prayer, Roger pursued Atkinson to Ellin Ashton's where he spoke his mind, declaring that standing at the gospel, with other ceremonies then in use, was merely Romanish foppery. Hereafter, declared Roger, since he could not come to the public ordinances without a scene, he would betake himself such receptacles (conventicles he meant) where he could serve God without disturbance. 'Ralph Winstanley, Atkinson[s'] disciple of the Black Tribe of Gad, came in and spoke his venom ... but I fly to God for refuge.' Standing up to vicars hoisted Roger's self-respect.

It will be seen that Roger's religion was not of a highly spiritual type. His Puritanism was a kind of theological partisanship. The puritan was given to meditation upon his spiritual successes and failures, he as inclined to dwell upon hours when he had been in touch with is God, or to lament days when the face of the Almighty was turned from him. His was a life of reflection. Emotion recollected in tranquillity was the poetry of his everyday life. There was emotion enough in Roger, but little recollection,, and no tranquillity, and consequently no beauty to poetry. There was no uplift to his faith, rather something immediately useful in time of defeat. 'God's providence', he wrote, 'is the poor man's inheritance.'

He was less puritan than an Nonconformist with some of the lower middle-class attributes that tended to gather round Nonconformity. He had that eagerness to do good, to improve his neighbours and in accordance with his own conceptions that we associate with the Nonconformists. Calling on his sister, Katherine, he 'advised her for her good to bethink herself live and godly, considering she had but a short time to live here'. His sister was naturally offended. Even more misplaced was his zeal in another instance. He went to look upon Anne Smith who had drowned her child, and was in hold presumably awaiting assizes. As the poor creature sat with hanging head by the chimney, Roger, not content with seeing her misery, exhorted her to repent and spoke of the mercifulness of God, who had pardoned David the adulterer and murderer.

To Roger's credit must be said that he recorded his own weaknesses, though not quite with the relish of Pepys in evil-doing. In spite of his church going, his ability to repeat sermons and his godly conversations with ministers, he could not always keep his mind on the services. During a sacrament, and a solemn occasion it was, his thoughts had been on Mary Barton who was sitting not far away. After an agreeable Sunday afternoon in the alehouse with friends from Leigh who had brought wenches with them, Roger wrote remorsefully: 'The Lord forgive us.' It was not wrong to visit a tavern between sermons, but to spend the whole Sunday afternoon in the company of young women, in other words to have too good a time on the Lord's day, was questionable. His conscience pricked him, too, when he had been drinking and felt the worse for it. He had a poor stomach from alcohol, and the day following a merry evening was frequently less than comfortable. With his headache he was likely to remember the Lord who 'instigated the pain.' Once, however, when he was sick for a day and a night from too much ale, the Lord relented to the extent of strengthening him.

It has been seen that Roger was easily emotional. He was fond of giving his emotions a quiet opportunity. Sometimes they played leapfrog within him, as when he wrote of a communion service: 'It was a joyful night and a sad night.' He found himself one day in the village of Leigh and betook himself with his sister to the churchyard to weep over the graves of his father and mother. Something there was about churchyards and their inhabitants not to be missed; they offered the chance to mourn over frailty and perishability of man. Roger was pleasantly moved by considering 'how one day houses, lands, goods, yes and friends and all will leave us'. It was Roger's version of 'Alas, poor Yorick'. He climbed to the top of the church steeple with John Hindley, and they 'discoursed of former days and passages past and gone'. They could have looked down on the churchyards; there was the grave of the Sanders Sixes and they could remember the day he broke his neck out riding. Another day Roger looked down from the steeple and watches the sexton digging a grave. Death was indeed terrible, but it had fascination. It was a subject not to be shunned, as we shun it today, but to be cherished. Roger had been told often enough by the minister that the sexton was not the last word, but save in his verses, where he is conventionally eager to leave his unhappy lot in this world and reach to friends in another, he was not interested in the other world.

His verse ought not to be mentioned, and yet he would have mentioned it, and it was part of him. His rhymes were hardly better than the average of village verse of his time, if as good. When writing to a friend who has failed him in correspondence, he added:

When I into your letter once did see
And be-held no remembrance of poor me,
Then to myself I said: 'Hodge thou'rt forgot,
For he in his letter Lowe remembers not.'

Eles Leland asked Roger to write a message for her to Thomas Smith, one of Roger's cronies, and Roger finished it off with:

Your friendship's like the morning's dew
No sooner come but bids adieu.
With other objects you are taken,
And little Hodge is quite forsaken.

After falling out with Emm Potter, Roger was low in his mind, and tried to translate his distress into verse. We will quote sparingly:

Let world say best and worse, all's one to me,
In time my quarrel will revenged be.
And they sat that are the actors of my grief
may they cry out and yet find no relief.

This must have sounded a little un-Christian, for Roger reconsidered:

But this I wish not: O, that they may be
Preserved from all such kind of misery.

If his shop duties and love affairs were both depressing him he indented some of the worse verse:

Thou whilst not suffer me long t' live in woe
Sure, Lord, thou'll come to visit poor Lowe.

Roger's confidence that the Lord would not allow him indefinitely to live in woe was not entirely justified. Shop matters became so pressing that he could think of little else. His relations with his master, Thomas Hamond, were giving him uneasiness. Hamond had always been considerate, and unusually inclined to be pleased with Roger's management of the shop, even when Roger feared that he was not doing well enough. But his master had probably picked up on some of the gossip about Roger and his love affairs, and warned his apprentice to be careful. From Chaddock, the apprentice in the shop at Leigh, and from others, Roger began to hear reports that his master proposed to move him to Leigh. It was a move that Roger dreaded, fearing perhaps that he would have less freedom there, and that he would be unable to gather in the extra shillings he gained in Ashton.

It is possible that his master believed him to be neglecting the shop on account of his preoccupation with Mary and Emm, and there would have been many in the community so to inform him. Roger may well have been away from the shop a good deal of the time and have given his best thoughts to matters other than buying and selling.

His own conscience, indeed, troubled him about a visit to a cock-fight or even and idle trip to Prescot or Wigan, though it may have been less his failure towards his master than the fear that he was standing in his own way. He was always excusing his expenditures at the alehouses, as if he knew only too well that sixpences were slipping through his fingers there, and that a lot of sixpences would be needed if he ever hoped to set up for himself.

There was probably more fundamental reasons for his dissatisfaction. He was spending his years without acquiring knowledge, as he called it, that is, the special kinds of business expertness that would enable him to get on. He had enough experience to understand the usefulness of special training and he was becoming increasingly sensitive about the humble nature of his post. He was angry one day in the alehouse when Nicholas Houghton, 'began to give disdaining words out against the art of a grocer or mercer, and so particularised it as to me'. This sensitiveness appeared, too, when he noted in his diary that someone had shown him great respect. It was egoism, but also an alertness in estimating his own position in the eyes of others.

We may guess that he had come into little from his parents. The brother who figures in the diary seems to have been desperately poor, and the one sister (there were two sisters, but we know little about the other one) and her husband were not much better off. Roger may have come from one of those families that have ability but no other inheritance to leave off their offspring.

It was no mean inheritance, but it did not serve to make him happy, rather to make him realise what he lacked. He had proved himself competent in his work, and he could not but compare himself with those more rich in fortune. 'I must confess I have a proud, envious spirit, seeing and thinking of others in their prosperity, and am apt to censure God for hard measure unto me.'

It was his way of saying that there was something wrong with a system that fixed one of his talent on so low a rung of the ladder, although, of course, he never thought of systems. Had he been a working man today, he would have deemed himself a victim of capitalism.

This humble position hurt him more because he realised that in spite of his attractiveness to women, he was regarded by their parents and even by the young women themselves in their harder Lancashire moments as no great catch. It was the distraction born of this realisation that perhaps made him a trimming adventurers in love. If God seemed about to provide a wife with a house and living, someone who could rescue him from his apprenticeship, who was he to frustrate the divine will with a n affair of the heart?

In his worry about his position he always flew to the Lord. His problem was to help Providence to solve his own inscrutable plan for himself. When he wrote: 'I was very sad all day, but the Lord is my comfort', we need not be concerned about his spiritual condition; his troubles were of this earth and he would not leave his God unenlightened about them. There were always minor troubles to be disposed of; the Lord's attention might be called a tedious stitch in his back, or to his inability to unsnarl his love tangles. But his major worry the Almighty was given little opportunity to overlook. 'When I came home I was very pensive and sad in consideration of my poverty, and I sung the 24th. psalm, and after I was very hearty.' Poverty it was and the ill-esteem that accompanied it, that irked this north-country lad. He tried to assure himself that 'they-re not so happy as have these worldly enjoyments', but that was tame cheer.

He could not be envious. 'Yet grudge not to see wicked men prosperous, it's but a while that shall flourish thus; prosperity will be hard pennyworth for them.' To see the rogues flourish and honest folk droop was no easier in his generation than in any other. But who were these wicked, one asks, that were to receive the hard pennyworth? Surely not the gentle families, whose tenants and servants were his associates; they scarcely impinged upon his world. Was he thinking of those among his own class on more rapidly than he, of the young men whom he assisted in their business affairs, whose wives he had wooed for them? His mood of malevolence towards his own associates seems less than gracious. It was a comfort to him to believe that God would punish them. That God was looking out in particular for him. 'God hath enough in store for me', he wrote, which was his peasant way of expressing his faith in his own star.

Yet more than once he had doubts. Was God inevitably on his side? Might it not be that his lack of success meant that God was angry with him? When such fears came upon him, he was likely to go out in the evening to Town Fields or the heath, and kneel in a ditch to indulge himself in long prayers. It was troubles with is master to blighted affection that brought him to the ditch, but his supplication dealt directly with the real cause of his discontent. And why to the ditch? There only was there privacy to pray.

Towards the end of his diary Roger's affairs suddenly took what seemed to be a turn for the better. In November 1665 his master offered to let him take over the goods on credit and go free. Roger was to take over the stock, paying for it as he could, and arrangements which, so far as we can judge without the details, seems to have been fair to Roger. He was now in command.

Roger began buying commodities on his own using credit with some of his old friends among merchants in the larger nearby towns. His difficulty was probably that he did not have long credit, as his master had had and that he found old debts to the shop impossible to collect. It is to be said for him that as soon as he gathered in any money he was quick to pay back his own debts. But it was not long before he found that being on his own was not what he had expected; his worries were increasing rather than diminishing. A noticeable sobriety crept into his diary from this time on, and much of the boyish disappeared. There were fewer visits to the alehouse, fewer descriptions of the idle love-making, more records of time spent seriously at work.

But in spite of his best efforts, things continued to go badly for him, and he finally handed the shop at Ashton back to his master and then entered service of Thomas Peake of Warrington, who had long wanted him in his shop. His wages were twenty pounds for three years. Mrs. Peake proved 'of such pestilential nature' that Roger was soon weary of this arrangement. It would appear that he went back eventually to Ashton. When he died in 1679 he left, in his house and shop, property appraised at sixty pounds, and probably owned the shop.

Long before that, however, he had felt certain enough for an income to be able to settle down to something more stable that his eternal friendship. Without the exuberance and wealth of detail that he had used in describing his romances, he announced his marriage to Emm Potter. He had sent Emm his 'designs and thoughts' in letters, thus making a conclusion of his 'overtired thoughts', and the two consummated their 'grand design of marriage' in 1668. Even before this date Roger was keeping his diary only intermittently and now it rapidly fades out. The last we see of him, he is still attending funerals, collecting debts, carrying marriage proposals from suitors to eligible women, and helping a neighbour to recover a stolen mare.

THE DIARY OF ROGER LOWE

OF ASHTON-IN-MAKERFIELD,

LANCASHIRE.

1663 -1678.

Including a record of burials at Winwick Church
1666-71.

Jenuery, 1662-3.

- i Friday.

Ann Barrow sent for me this morneinge. I went and stayed all day. I was somethinge sickley yet all day I was feareing the exceptance of love and att last she vouchsafed a time for consideracion. This evening when I came home I answerd an Invitation and went to Thomas Heyes and should have beene there all night but would not, came home at 1 or 2 a clocke in night.

Roger Lowe commences his diary with an entry relating to one of his courting expeditions. Love affairs were frequently the subjects which he considered worth noting in his diary, and some of the incidents are as amusing as they are innocent and simple.

- 2. Saturday.

I was sent for to Robert Rosbotham and was all night and ...

- 3 day. lords day.

We came to chappell, Mr. Madocke preached. I was ingaged in the Alehouse att a wedding of Isibell Hasleden, and promised to go into Reinford with them.

The diarist, it is clear, from almost his first entry was a young man of pious inclinations; but what must strike the reader as very incongruous if the frequent reference in almost the same paragraph to religious matters and the ale-house. Whenever friends met or had any business to transact it might be natural that the ale-house was resorted to, but after divine service, both morning and evening, a visit to the tavern was not uncommon and sometimes the clergy man even accompanied his hearers and had a glass at their expense!

- 4. Lords day.

I was envited to go with Thomas Tickle and his wife to Reinford. John Hasleden went with me. We rid of puplies (?) 2 mares. The reason for our going was to avince to old Sephon the young couple's marriage. We came thither and the old man seemed to be displeased but it was awhile. The next day.

- 5. Tusday.

We went to chappell to Lawrence Gaskell's and spent each man 4d. but old man payd all. Thence we went to Barringtons and did likewise. It began to be late and I desired to go home and moved John Hasleden to go. Old man plaid upon me which made me willinge to goe but John would not go being invited by his unkle to stay. I pted came home myself in darke night a very sad night and as I came in Ashton near Widow Marshes old James Hanys lived over against and was newly drowned.

- 6. Wedensday.

My brother cald on me to go with hime to take a house and ground near Pisley Windy mill but we tooke none. We mett Cozen Hugh Lowe went to alehouse I spent 6d. and soe parted.

-7. Thursday.

I went this night to Thomas Heyes on purpose to read over some writeinge for hime.

- 10. Lords day.

John Bradshawe came form Leigh to see me. I was very sad all day but the Lord is my comfort.

- 14.

John Battensbie, sometime Leigh's schoole-master, came to towne, and I was with him all night and ...

- 19. Jenuery tusday.

I went to Goleborne to James ... for to gett in some moneys from thence I went to Ann Barowes and I suposd she hid her selfe att last I pted from house and she came after me but I returned home with discomfort tho I was very much satisfied for I went with purpose to free myself and not to have nothing to doe with her.

- 26. Tusday.

John Parr of Tilsley Bangs beyond Leigh came to town and forced me with him to go to Alehouse which I did and it cost me nothinge. I was at this time very sad in spirit.

The local name of Tilsley-Bongs if forshadowed in the diary. The descriptive name of Tyldesley Banks had evidently two centuries ago become corrupted into unmeaning words.

ffebruery, 1663.

- Wednesday.

I was all day indeavouringe to rectifie some things between old John Jenkins and his soun Matthew who ware att suite the one against the other and a peace was concluded and all things rectifide in and amongst them. We all went to the Alehouse together and I made Bond for to pay such a sum of moneys att such a time and so parted.

2

- Thursday.

Rogr Taylor and Richard Twisse and would have me go with them to Alehouse. I went and very mery we were. I must not spend a 1d. but yet I did.

- 5th. Friday.

I was much troubled about a business that befell about writeing a letter for Ellin Ashton to her son Charles. She related that I writt to have her sonne come down that she knew not of which was a false lye.

- 6. Saturday.

This morneinge I went to Ellin Ashtons and spent 2d. and peace was concluded which was mattr of great satisfaction to my mind.

- 8th. Munday.

I went to Thomas Hollys and William Chadockes to buy swines grasse, which I did, and when I came home I was very pensive and sad in consideration of my povertie, and I sunge the 24th psalme, and after I was very hearty god will comfort and suply the wants of his poor servants ...

March, 1662-3.

- i Lords day.

Att night I being somewhat sad, resorted to Ashton towne Heath, and there pourd out a prayr to god, bring aside of a ditch. Att my returne I found Thomas Smith and he would have me goe to Mr. Woods which we did but I stayd not. Mr. Woods lent me a booke.

The diarist's puritanical turn of mind manifests itself throughout the diary, and often in connection with matters and things pious expressions are introduced in almost a riduclous manner. Nonsensical and trivial as these entries may appear now, they throw much light on the character of Roger Lowe, and show him to have been deeply inbuded with the peculiar religious tone of the time in which he lived.

- 7th. Saturday.

I was sent for to Christopher Bate to Brinn and I went and very Jollyfully to my Joy I was payed the debt oweing to me by Mr. Brunkes and very Jollyfully I came home.

- ii. Wednesday.

My Mr. came to Ashton, and I was halfe afraid of his angr, but the Lord turned it to best, for the great deale to me which did very much rejoice. The Lords name be magnifide.

-15. Lords day.

Att after evening prayr there was a few went to Mr. Woods to spend the remaing part of theday. I repented, ... and stayed prayer, and then came our way.

The 'Mr. Woods' referred to is the Rev. James Woods, the ejected Nonconformist minister of Ashon. He was the grandfather of 'General Woods' of Chowbent, and the father of the then minister of the Chowbent Presbyterian Chapel.

- 17. Tusday.

I went to the funerall of a child ... When we came to Winwicke I went with John Hasleden James Jenkins Ann Hasleden Margaret Sankrfield Ann Taylor to Mr. Barkrs to heare Organes. I never heard any before, and we ware very mery. I spent 6d. and see we came home.

- 22. Lords day night.

I went to Mr. Woods stayd prayr and Edmund Winstanley wuld have me home with him to suppr and I went with him.

24. Tusday.

I went to Leigh.

- 29. Lords day.

Went with John Hasleden to Wiggin and when I came home I was scarcely well. We stayed drinking at Beony Bourdekins house.

April 1663.

- 5. Lords day.

I was in a troubled condition in my mind considring my unsettlednes and that god was highly offended with me therfor I went into Ashton Heathes and kneeled me downe in a ditch and made my prayr to the Lord.

-6. Munday.

Old Mr. Woods went to Chewbent and I brought hime on his way.

This is an interesting entry, as it was easy to divine the cause of the old Puritan minister's visit to Chowbent - spelt by the diarist in the old form. No doubt many Chowbent people remembered the visit, and knew the young man from Ashton who 'brought' the old pastor 'on his way.'

-9. Thursday.

Mr. Woods returned again and cald on me and told me where he had beene and how he had made peace between Mrs. Duckewilde of Bickerstaffe and her

4

son James he seemed to be very glad. I went to bring him towards home and he told me he light of a recite for diseases since he went and puld out a papr and lent me to write out I told him he had made it himself, as I supose he did this it was.

An healinge receit for a diseased liver ffirst fast and pray and then take a quart of repentance of Ninivah and put handfulls of faith in the blood of Christ and as much hope and charitee as you can gett and put it into a vessell of a clean consience then boile it on the fire of love so longe till pale by ye eyes of faith a blacke scum of ye love of the world ... then scum it off cleane with ye spoone of faithful prayrs. When this is done put the powder of patience then straine together in ye cupp of a humble heart then drinke it burnening hott next thy heart to cover thee warme with as many clothes of amendment of life as God shall enable thee to bear and that though maist sweat out all the poyson of wantones pride whoredome idolatrie usury swearing lyeing with such like and when thou feelest thy selfe altered from the afore-named vices take ye poder of say well and put it upon thy tongue but drinke it with thrice as much of do well daily then take the oyle of good workes and anoint therwith eyes, eares heart hands that thou be readie and nimble to ministr to ye poor distressedmembers of Xt. When this is done then in god's name arise from sin willingly read in the bible daily take up the cross of Xt. boldly and stand to it manfully bear and visitations patiently pray continually rest thankfully and thou shalt live everlastingly and come to the hill of joy quickly to which place hasten us good lord speedily.

This receipt is written in a style of overstrained allegory very common to the times, and of which instances may be found in most of the writings of the Puritans, and notably in the 'Pilgrims Progress' and the other works of John Bunyan.

-12. lords day.
Being commanded by my Mr. to come to Leigh I went and measure was taken on me for a suit of clothes att noone my Mr. and I went to see his child which was nursed at Morles. From thence we went to John Hindley upon Mosse side ... was sicke but our cheife occasion was to se John Chadocke who lyde sicke att Mr. Whiteheads in Astley. We stayed awhile then we came home and I came to Ashton.

Morley's Hall, in Astley, was the seat of the Leylands in the reign of Henry VIII., and was described by Leyland, the antuquary. It is now merely a farm house.

-13. Munday.
I went to Warrington to buy comodities.

-15. Wednesday night.
I went to Mr. Woods to be all night Mr Woods had a private day of prayr he would not have had me to have come at but I said I durst not.

5

-23. Thursday.

Mr. Woods came to take leave of every inhabitant and cald upon me I went with hime and with great lamentation at his going with advise to every family to live well.

This is a simple and touching record of the parting of the ejected minister with his old congregation and friends. After Mr. Woods left Ashton he went to reside at Thelwall, near Warrington.

-24. Friday.

John Woods came to shop and gave me these verses followeing being made by a minister in prison a non-conformist.

Though I am shutt from thy house and my one [own]
I both enjoy in thee my gd alone
ffirst for thy servant I to prison went
Now for thy son to prison I am sent
For biden prairs was my reason then
For that was Daniell cast in't lyons denn
The wheel is turnd preaching is now my crime
Was it not so in th' apostles time
rejoice my soule and be exceeding glad
such measure in old time ye prophets had
Paull in his hired house in bonds did preach
in neither I pmitted am teach
father blest be thy name thy [kingdom] come
thy will be done though I remaine dumbe --

The remainer of these singular verses is illegible and very obscure.

-Lords day.

I went to Mr. Wood's house with Thomas Smith stayed prayer it was the last lords day night that Mr Woods stayed in Ashton he intended to goe to Cheshire to live he preacht amongst us out of ye 14 psalme 5 verse the lord is my refuge very much affected he was with parteing with Ashton, gave him 12s. bended[?] but he would take no leave of me for he thought to see me often.

-30. Thursday.

I went to Leigh to my geat greefe my Mr. tooke on me 3li that I had gotten with writeinge and had given me when I have lived as in Warrington Lirple [Liverpool?] ... I was sent for to Whitleige greene this night to one William Marsh who lay sicke and had seaverall times sent for me to write his will which I did. John Hasleden went with me in [the] night and William Knowle was there and I composed the mans will somewhat handsomely.

6

May 1663.

-3. lords day.

Att noone Thomas Smith and severall young women was assembled togather in fields and I repeated sermon. I was this day somewhat pensive this day by reason of some greevences that ware upon my spirit.

-5. tusday.

Being envited to goe to Banfer longe to Ann Greinsworth I was in Rogr Naylors and word was sent me my Mr. was pasd to shoppe soe I went after and overtooke him but he was not offended afterwards I went to Banfer longe. Att my comeing home I cald att Rogr Naylors and partly ingaged to come beare them company at night I comeing down to shope and stayed awhile and then went againe and privately ingaged to Mary to sit up awhile to let us discource which she promised and the maine question was because we lived seaverally that we wuld not act soe publikely as othrs that we might live privately and love firmly that we might be fathfull to each other in our love till the end, all which was firmely agreed upon. This was the first night that I ever stayed up wooing Ere in my life.

-12. tusday.

My Mr brought me a suite of clothes which did much comfort me.

-14. Thursday.

I was envited to goe to the funerall of Edward Calland to Winwicke which I did.

-17.

I was to goe to Wiggin with Thomas Smith. Ales leyland had promised me she would then and there answr my desire either pro or con in finalising ingaement to Thomas att this time Mary Naylor and I were solemnly agreed to be faithfull to each othr.

-20. Wednesday.

John Chadocke came to Ashton to help cast up shop and it answrd my expectation. I desired to bless God for it for the Lord hath beene pleasd to blesse it hitherto in my handes.

-30. Sabath day.

I went to Wiggan and should have mett John Chadocke but he came not.

June 1663.

-3. Wedensday.

I was envited to Mr. Leandrs house and I went att my comeing home I mett with Mr. Leandrs and he have me to Ale house.

-4. Thursday.

I went to the funerall of old Mrs. Duckenfield first to Bickershawe then to Wiggen I thought I should have mett with Mr. Hayhurst and Mr. Downes but they were not there. I came considering how one day houses lands goods and friends and all will leave us as I particularised it to her that was dead.

-5. Friday.

I was adopted to be sonn and twindle with Richard Bendman of Ashton ... we ...

-6. Saturday.

I made 3 bonds for old Jenkins.

-8. Munday.

I went to Rogr Naylor and Mary cryd to me said she would have nothing to doe with me was highly displeased att me but in the conclusion she was well pleased would have me goe with her aftr to Banfer longe and she would goe before and to signifie she was before she would in such a place lay a bough in the way which accordingly she did and I found it upon.

-9. Tusday.

Before goeing to Banfor longe and att house I found her as we came home we went into a narrow lane and spoke our minds walkeing to and fro and ingaged to be faithfull till death. As we ware comeing I saw John Chadocke goeing home haveing beene att Ashton bringeinge me a parcell of cloth. I cald one hime and get hime backe againe.

-15. Munday.

A tedious stich tooke in my backe so yt I was unable to stay shop and held me very sore till noone and then the lord helped me.

-16. Tusday.

I was sent for to Runners feld to be all night out I went out.

-17.

I was envited to goe with Sarah Jenkins to John Naylors of Edge greene.

-21. lords day.

I went to Leigh and there Mr. James Woods came into church was lately maried Thursday before and his wife was now with hime and att noone I went into George Norris where he was sent for hime into chambr where I was and when he came he sent for his wife that I should see her. At night I came to Sushey(?) and there I mett with Margarett Wright Mr Sorow colds maid she needs would have me with her at home. I went and she made much of me. I came from thence to Rogr Naylors and there they ware att supr. I went with Mary and othr wenches to a well bottome of towne field.

-22. Munday.

I heareing that old Mr. Woods was at John Robinsons I hastened to goe see him hime which I did. there we sate and discoursed awhile of the times and they tooke theire leaves of house and I went with them they intending to call at Neaw Hall and there I left them being greeved in spirit.

-24. Wedensday.

I went into Windle to my brothers and he was gone to Warrington. I went and fished a little time but catchinge nothing I came home.

-28. Sabath day.

There was no service att Ashton and I came to Banfor longe and stayd awhile and came home again I promised to ... Ellin Scott ...

July 1663.

-5. lords day.

After meny envitations to goe with Ellin Scott to Holland this day I answered her envitation and went to Banfor longe where she lived and get her readie. so we went to Holland togethr and when we came there it was befor service time we went to Hugh Worthington and spent 2d. so went into church a younge lad preachd. att noone we went to her mothers in Dorton stayd diner then Elizabeth Scott livd att Ashurst Hall and she tooke us downe thithr as we ware goeinge we looked up and downe stood upon a hill and saw the land round about its the pleasent place that Ere I saw almost gallant prospect. Came to Ashurst Hall and Elizabeth tooke us into the chambrs up and downe a most plesasant place and gallant walks we envited Elizabeth fellow servant to goe take part of half a dozen which was done we went togathr to one Ashcroft and as we went we gat Winbery from thence we parted and came home.

-8. Wedensaday.

I was in a sad condition in mind for Roge Naylor was from home and Mary would not assent to have me come thithr but I went and she was something displeased. She went give Calfe drink I followed her and there we speake to eithr which was very satisfactory to both and the other day aftr she came to shopp and was

9

very glad to see me she said she am not I a wise wench to ingage myselfe thus at these times my effections ran out violently after so as that i was never contented one day to an end unless I had seene her and cheefly my effections were sett upon her vertues and womanly qualities.

-13. Munday.

I went to Leigh for comodities and my Dame was brought to bed she sent for me into parler for to get some wine from Ashton. I said I would come againe and bring her some tooke my leave and came home. I was sent for to Banfer longe to Ann Greinsworth to write letters to London and Preston tooke my leave and came to Rogr Naylors house the cabinet yt received the choice of me effection her father was not att home and she gave me a handhrcheife because I was hott to dry me with. I went and brought wine and set forward to Leigh when then thithr I went to see my sister and Robert Reynolds went & gave me half a dozen lent me his watch the othr day I came home and when comen I went to Rogr Naylors and there Mary was put in fright with her father concerning me for which shee reserved the telling of it till another time but it was mattr of much trouble to me. I was sent for to Banfer longe and I went but it was with sad heart for I sincerely loved her - and now what a greefe is it yt such a miserable friend as love is such a friend as is desired every where and without a common weale nay a family would not subsist yet that this friend that we two have made choice above all othrs yet that there should be such actrs and abettrs aginst it as her father and othrs some my .. others may let hime remaine silent in ye cabinet of our hearts and indeed thats or resolution till mallice and frite have said theire worst and best and then weele advance this our friend to the highest protection till then we will be silent.

The diarist's courting appears to have been very checkered. The diary commences with a reference to one of his sweethearts, and many entries refer to Mary Naylor. On the 30th. August following the above entry, Lowe hints that he was 'prosecuting his service' to a 'lady with means' and after these varied experiences, as the sequal proves, he does not after all marry one of his early sweethearts.

-15. Wedensday.

I sent to Tho. Smith undr hand to Mary to know the buisnes so the busines was litle she was put in affright and sent for me to come the other day.

-16. Thursday.

I went and we went into parler and very sorow fully we ware att some buisnes. We concluded to be more privat and Keape more faithful.

-16. Thursday.

Att night James Naylor came and asyed me to goe with him to Neawton which I did. He wood Ann Barrow and she sen for us to Stirrops where we came and get into chambr where she was and after a while parted.

-18. Saturday.

I set forward to go to Thellwall in Cheshire to old Mr. Woods for I had promised him to come and as I was going in Warrington I went into Mr. Pickering shop and stayd awhile for it rained. I bought a book of Mr. Loves being his last sermon. I sat forward and upon Latchford Heath there was a great compeny of persons with 2 drums amongst the youg men ware playing at prison barrs where I stayed awhile to see them but concluded it was but vanitie. Came to Mr. Woods where they ware glad to see me.

The game of prison bars of base ball is an old English game. The one witnessed on Lathford Heath by the diarist appears to have been somewhat of a match, much as friendly games of cricket are played now, with the similar attraction ofmusic to encourage the players and entertain the spectators.

-19. lords day.

We went altogeather to Limme church and...

-20th. Munday.

I came home.

-22. Wedensday.

Richard Naylor came over and sent for me so I went and we went to Leeches I spent 6d. att night James Naylor asked me to goe with him to Neawton as formrly so I went and stayd awhile anon Mr Collirs so we went and stayd awhile anon Mr. Collir comes in drunke and falls in discourse with James and James being not able to defend himselfe I tooke hold and answerd to the well likeing of James.

-25.

I rid upon one of Ralph Hasleden horses to Leigh to our child's christennige he was named Edward.

According to the registers, no christenings took place at Leigh Church on the above date, but Edward, son of Thomas Hamond de Westleigh, was baptized July 26. The only other Edward babtized in the same month was Edward, son of Thomas Suthern de Bedford, on the 19th.

August 1663.

-i. Saturday.

I went to Winwick to the funerall of old John Tankerfield. I hasted home and went to see Mary Naylor for she was scarce well being troubled with toothache.

11

-2. lords day.

Mr. Wood sent for me into Hadicke to Nicholas Burscoes where Thomas Smith and I went and stayd and so came home.

-9. friday.

Old Mr Woods came to towne to me and Peter Lealand William Knowles William ... ware altogather in Alehouse very merry.

-9. lords day.

Matthew Lythgo Edward Bradshaw Robert Reynolds came from Leigh sent for me to Tankerfields and had wenches that mett them. we ware alt aftrnoone in ale house the lord forgive us.

-12. Wedensday night.

We were all to gather in Thomas Leeches taking leave with Thomas Greene haveing his apprnticshipe ended.

-18. Wedensday.

Richard Naylor came ovr out of Yorkshire and Henry Lowe and I were with him very mery and ware adopted bretheren.

-19. Wedensday.

I was sent for to Banfor longe to cast up Annes accounts.

-12. Thursday.

I was in alehouse with Rogr Naylor when we parted. I was somewhat effected and betooke myself soliterily into Townes feild and kneeld me downe on side of a came butt and prayd.

-23. lords day.

Att night Tho Smith and I went to Robt Rowbothams to be all night [for] the other [next] day.

-24.

Robert gat us plumes we hastened away from there was a race to be run from Goleborne Stockes to Ashton towne. I gat a horse and Ran with them.

- 28. Friday.

I went to Wiggan there was a pedler lived there one Humphrey Starbotham who ought me some monys but I gat none.

-29.

Thomas Smith and I went to Edward Clarkes to be all night as soone as we ware gotten into house he told us that Ales Lealand was lately dead that evening a very godly young woman.

-30. lords day.

Mary Naylor frowned one me all day and I was very much troubled to know the reason and cause of it so I went into house and att my returne homeward I went to bring Ann Greinsworth towards home and at my returne homeward I went into house and found her alone and wild her to tell me the reason for her fowneinge but she would not but I was very much troubled att it but I comitt all to God for my trust in hime. I had before this time prosecuted my service to Ellin Marsh of Ashton and who had a house and liveinge and kept a private mediator to intercede for me from whom and by whome I received answr that she would give me the meeting ere longe onely I must be secret to which I promised I would. The lord worke for me which way may be most for his glory and my comfort and direct me what best to take in hand and order all my effaires.

September 1663.

-1. Munday.

Rogr Naylor was gone to Chestr and I went downe and Mary and I went into parlour and talked 2 howres att least and she cryd to me and seemed to be very sad and the reason was because of fear of her friends lest they would never respect her so she would have us part. I was endifferent tho' sadly troubled but ere we parted she was very mery bec. she had eased her spirit to me so we parted but is was with a further resolution of failthful and constant effection.

-2. tusday.

Ellin Ashton came to me to write a letter for her which I did. Att this present I was very much discomposed in spirit being troubled in mind in considracion of my poorness in the world but my trust in in god for the earth is his and the fullness therof.

-4. Thursday.

It was a very rainy day and I went with William Sixsmith and John Pottr to Whitleigh greene. My intentions ware to see some that owed moneys to get it and come home againe but we went into Watts and spent each man 2d. and made a sett of Bowleinge for each man 2d. in ale. I was one to bowle and lost and came home shutt up windowes and went againe and found them in house get mony that I had lost and came home but a sad evening and a sad day of sickness I had afterwards.

Bowling is another ancient English game and is represented in Anglo-Saxon illuminated MMS. The customary 'twopence a game for ale' appears to be very Conservatine Institution, and the same stake is probally the usual one still played for on the Bowling Greens of Ashton two centuries after Roger Lowe records the sad evening he had in consequence of loosing a game, and how he had a 'sad day of sickness' the following morning.

-6. lords day.

My Mr. came to towne and was something displeas'd I came not to Leigh for a lords day but he was not ovr much angry but very well pleased with me and he went to dock lane to dinr. Att night I being very sad in spirit went to Towne feild and up and down att last I get to Towne heathe and upon a ditch side I read a psalme and sunge part of another and came home being very well satisfied for the lord will be a rocke to those that trust in hime.

-10. Thursday.

I was sent for to Banfer longe to Ann Greinsworth to write and it was a very Rainy day. This day Hamblett of Ashton was att Warrington buryd being munday before hangd at Chestr for murdr the lord preserve us from such practices and such end. Amen.

In the Warrington Register, under the date of September 10, 1663, occurs the entry; 'Mr. Hamellett Ashton Buried.' It appears that he was hanged for killing a tapster at Nantwich.

-13. lords day.

I went to Leigh and att noone John Bradshaw and I went into Vicars field and talked of formr things. I was at this time very sad in spitit by reason of my selfe and seeing my fathers and mothers grave and pondering of other deaths for I went round about church to looke at graves of such as I knew.

The Vicarage Fields retain their name, but the graves of the diarist's parents cannot be pointed out in the Parish Church-yard.

-15. tusday.

Mr. Woods came to shop to see me and he told me of his sadnes for Eles Lealands death and he delivrd to me a paper of verses that he had made and gave me them to write out and willd me to come this evening to Bates in Hadocke he would be there this night and I promised I would come to hime as soone as I had writt them.

Some verses I composed upon the sad and serious thoughts of Elice Lealand's death,

Ann Epitaph upon the death
Of Elice Lealand maid of Ashton
who dyed 29 of August 1663.
And was buryd 30 August att Ashton Chappall
being lords day in the evening and these
verses were made by Mr. James Woods
Senior and was given to me to write out

by hime 15. September 1663.
Dear Alice though thy portion was but small
In Riches beauty things terrestriall
Yet of the in ward beauty thou hadest share
thy soule ad ornaments ware both great & rare
wt others had in out ward garbe and blee
in in ward graces was made up to thee
O blessed saint though though wast poor and meane
thy life was gracious conversation cleane
thou much of heaven hadst of earth but little
though hadst the sollid wantedst but the britle
Of outward wealth and ti tles though hadst none
like Xt nor house nor harbor of thy own
though scarcely hadst an hole to hide thy head
yet wantest not a pallace being dead

....

Yes to expresse my true respects to thee
these verses here a monument shall be
we may phaps not without tears he read
when I as well as thou am buried
and I doe hope yt longe it will not be
but I (blest saint) shall blessed be with [thee]

Sic finitur lacrimationes

| 15 Septembr | ami corum | Jacobus Woods |
| 1663 | | Rogerus Lowe.. |

        After I had written this I sett forward according to my promise to follow him and att Henry Bates in Haydocke I found him att prayr for Henrys sister was distempered. As soone as he could leave them we walked 2 feilds beadth and parted both being very sad. I came to old John Rob ... they would have had me to have eaten but ... stayd awhile and then parted onely I let hime se 4 verses I made upon his not rememberance of me in a letter to Ashton which I had intended to have written a lettr and sent it to hime.

When I into your letter once did see
an bee-held no rememberance of (poor me)
then to myself I said Hodge thou'rt forgot
for he in his lettr Lowe remembereth not
att the reading of which he laughed heartily.

15

These 'verses' occupy nearly three pages of the diary and extend to about 130 lines. The portion re-printed will give a fair idea of their 'poetic' merit. The Leylands were settled at a very early date in Ashton-in-Makerfield, and an offshoot of the original stock subsequently took root in Abram.

-17. thursday.

I went to bowling Alley and lost 12d att which I was sore greeved came home and this evening I went with James Naylor to Neawton a wooing Ann Barrow she had sent for me to come speake with her. I went to Mr. Collirs to fetch her to us into widow Heapys for there we reside. I put of my one hatt and put on another and made also my as if I ware John Naylors man and was sent to towne upon occasion and so had something to speake to Ann from her sister. Get her out and she with much requesting promised to come to us after supper which shee did desird me to meete her att Winwick lords day after.

-17. friday.

I helpt att the desire of old John Jenkins to picke sheaves of Barley of cart.

-18.

I was in a great p'plextie by reason of Mary Naylor who ws too strange to me in her effections.

-19. lords day.

I went to Winwicke with James Naylor to mett Ann Barrow accordinge to my promise. I went but she could not come. We came to Heapys at noone and stayd drinking 8d. then set for by her we went into Mr. Collirs and taken into the parlour and I conferred with her awhile to move her acceptance after awhile I left her and hime to their best discourse.

-21. Munday.

John Bradshaw came from Leigh to see me and we went to Gawthers and drunke and then afterwards went to Brinnne to see a race but it was run before we came so we came to shop againe.

-22. tuday.

Nicholas Corles of Abreham came to towne to me took to Alehouse. I went and brought hime a gate towards home and so parted. This night Mary Naylor came to me and spake kindly to my great satisfaction this night John Hasleden was pretty merry and he goes to John Pottrs and sends 6d for ale and sent for me it was made in a jelly bowle and I was sent for to the drinkeing of. Att this time I was neither merry nor sad but in an endifferant state rather in greefe but the Author of my faith and hope is fixed in god he can he will redeeme me out of all my feares and greefes I shall see better times wherin I shall have further ... the lord.

16

The name originally of the family and township of Abram was Edburgham or Adburgham and the name Richard de Edburgham is found in the Testa de Neville of the thirteenth century. The name at the time of the diarist was variously spelt, Abraham, Abreham and Abram.

-24. Thursday.

Eles Lealand came form Mr. Woods in Cheshire I brough her towards home we talked of Eles lealans death. In the close of her discourse she desired me to do a message for her to Tho Smith from Mr. Woods wh I promised I would - and because Thomas seldome came to shop and I could not see him I writt the Arrend downe to him and in bottome of pag I made and writt these verses

Your friendships like the morneings deaw
No sooner comme but bids adieu
with other objects you are taken
and little Hodge is quite forsaken
but I'me content it be soe
though friends will nere freinds them put fro

This afternooon I went down to Rogr Naylors and Mary and I talked togeather. After she and I ware parted James and I went to Leashe and when I came home there was a direct N and halfe of M provedentially made upon my breeches plaine to view in any mans sight made of mire with leaping. I looked upon it to be from providence and fortold something in my aprhension. The smallest of gods providences should not be past by without observation.

The 'smallest of God's providences' is probally the most amusing entry in the diary. Lowe, in his love for Mary Naylor, was willing to see not only good, but Providence in everything which seemed to confirm his affection.

-25. friday.

I went to Rogr Naylors and Rogr was gone to Wiggan to a burying and poor Mary was sicke in bed I went to her and hild and stayd awhile she promised to send Joseph to tell me how she did. I parted and when I came to shop Ralph Stirrope my father send for me to Gawthrs I went.

-26.

Petr Lealand came and I writt Mr. Woods verses for hime. This night there was a Robery done att Clay pitts a young man was stricken of horse very kindly in night and his monys taken from hime.

-27th.

I went Leigh and gave Mr 5li 10s at my comeing home Margaret Naylor cald of me and ... me to come to their house when John Naylor was away. Att

17

this time I was somwt greeved in mind by reason I saw not those smiling providences of god as others but its good to waite on God.

-28. Munday.

John Hasleden and I with some others were in Tankerfeilds and ware merry. John and I began to bett each with other which was contrarie to custome that we should so act one against another.

-29.

James Naylor envited me to their house. I went and found Mary alone and very pleasant -- this night I sange in shopp by candle the cheife verses of .. psalme with a lusty heart chearfullness.

October 1663.

-1. Thursday.

I had goods sent fom Leigh in a cart being come from Chestr faire and was in a very harty condition.

-2. friday.

I went to Rogr Naylors and Mary and I sate togather in parlour and discoursed to bothe our satisfaction. I came to shop and anon John Chadocke came and brought me some comodoties and told me that my Mr intended to have me home and that some of his ladds should be set up in Ashton all which greeved me extremely but its best to fly to the helpe that nevr fails and to hold one still waiting one God he who hath brought me through infancie and youth will not now leave me nor forsake me for my trust is in hime.

-3. saturday.

I ecqueinted Mary Naylor with my thoughts about these former things above said about my departure from Ashton att she was greeved and would have me speake to my Mr. I was all this day sad yea very sad in heart but theres a god to comfort a discomfortable soule when we see nothing in ourselves but miserie nor nothing in world but trouble then looke up wards to God I will looke up into the Lord I will awaite one the god of me salvation my god will heare me. I went this evening with James Naylor to Newton to Ann Barrow a wooing. She had been sicke.

-4. lords day.

My brother came to Ashton. I told himme how that my Mr intended to take me home he was sorry in ye thinge but hoped all might be for best.

18

-5. Munday.

Mary Naylor sent for me to their house. We talked togeathr conderneing or privat matters and this morneing she promised nevr to marry except myself.

-6. day tusday.

I was sent for to Thomas Heyes to reckon with them and they owed me 3s. 10d. and I said 2s. 10d. but was mistaken.

-7. Wednesday.

I sent them this day. My Mr sent litle Thomas to me for to teach which greeved me very sore.

-8. thursday.

William Schofield a mercer in Warrington came to Ashton and envited me to goe with him to alehouse where I did and we talked about tradeinge and how to gett wives.

-11. lords day.

It was rainy day and I was very negligent in my duty to God the Lord forgive me.

-12. Munday.

I had a packe of candles came from Leigh. I was somewhat merry at this time in consideracon of Mary Naylors love to me the concideration thereof amidst othr greefes yet that is comfort to me and much rejoices me spirit in sadness.

-13. tuesday.

I sat in shop all day. Onely I went up greene to old parson Lees and John Haselden and Thomas Rosbothom and we all went to gether resting. Thomas Rosbothom and John Haselden attempting with either of them a good kibbas (?) to suprize poor parson and I in the parsons shop but we defended ourselves a while but in conclusion I was glad to creepe up into a loft to secure myselfe and was taken att last and fastened efliction(?) I made them to laugh in telling them how once I was hurried with a tupp in a Rope who comeing towards Leigh with Tupp in fields the tupp sett upon poor Hodge and so geper knowd (?) me that in the conclusion I cryd out but none heard me and I being oncequented how to act with tuppe in Rope let hime have the length of Rope and tupp ran all wayes backwards and fell one me so that I was put in a terrible fright what to doe to save my shinnes. I was almost in a bewailed condition. I layd me down with my head upon my leggs thinking to save me leggs and he gave me such a patt on the head made me turn up white eyes. I thought and was halfe efraid lest I had gotten old nicke in the Rope. I prayed to god to delivr me from the tupp and Rope but in the conclusion my bones ware sore brains sicke and heart dead with feare what to do with tupp. I looked at tupp with an angry countenance but could not tell how to be revenged. Kill him I durst not then I should have the labour to have carryd himme which I could not. Faire words would not pacifie him nor angry countenacnces efright him but att last I resolved upon a resolution thus. - What Hodge art in a streite whats the reason of thes feare and greefe a tupp a tupp does that daunt thee stand upon thy leggs and fight manfully in answer thereunto. I did and gett a kibbow out of the hedge and tupp and I fell to it but the tupp orecame me. I could doe no good but downe on my knees againe. I get hold of tupps horns and one of his feet and cast him. So now tupp I intend to be revenged on thee and smote him on the head but with great difficultie. I get him to Leigh but I nere was in such a puckle in all my life as I was with the tupp. When I saw the tupp set upon me so I thought what have I gotten on Rope a sheep is a harmeless creature they say. What is this old nicke he did so micke me up that he made me leap and skippe. I exercised feet hands tongue and all members of my body was exercised about tupp head. Sometimes slaked in revenge braines how to be revenged toungue in uttering most wofull lamentations and sometimes loud bankerings but since then I have knowne tupps the very name of tupps hath been trouble to me eares. I remember another story which once was to my greefe as well as this which occasions me to remember it. Likewise that the world may see what streits I have beene in and what troubles I have undergone in my life. When I lived with Mr. Livesley he sent me to High Lee to Mr. Henry Lee about a minister for his chappell and going from Budworth to High Lee without victuals I came just att dinrs time. Mr. Lee was att dinner. I sent a lettr to him he sent word I should stay diner which I did and was very hungery. I was sett att table with servants every servant a great bowleful of porrige anon a great trencher like a pott lid I and all others had with a great quantity of porrige. The dishes els ware but small and few. I put bread into my porrige thinking to have a spoone but none came while I was thus in expectation of that I could not obtain everyman having horne spoone in their pocket having done their pottage fell to the other dishes. Thought I these hungery Amallakites that I am gotten amongst I looking towards them to see their nimbleness in the exercise of their hands from their dish to their mouth made me to forget my hunger but I cast my eyes from them thinking it ware best to be thinke myself of my one hungery condition. What would it advantage me though I was sat there to table and not satisfie hunger. I cast an eye to my trencher there was a whole sea of pattage before thought I it must I dee with all those wished in my hart many times that those hungery rogues had them in their gutts but what that would not doe for still they ware there before me and I durst not set them away tho it was manurs so to have done. Well I resolved Hodge if thou will have any victualls here thou sees how the case is and into whose compeny thou art falne into what a hungery spirit possesses these men thou must now resolve upon action and a speedy dispatch with these pottage accordingly I did and swoped them as if I would have drunke. Than when I had them in my mouth I was in such a hott fitt in my mouth turned meditated into action but att last my lamentation I was worse then before. I would gladly have given 5s. that I had but had the benefitt of aire or anorthena (?) blast my tongue in my mouth was in a sad condition helpe myself I could not for table was before me and a wall behind me upon my backe a women with her flasket upon right hand and a man with his codd peece upon the other and in this sad condition I sat blothering knew not wt to doe best -- those few pottage I tasted was both diner and supper. I att last rise from table with a hungry belly but a lamenting heart and ere since I have been cautious how to supp pottage an likewise wary. Nothing worser to a man then over bussiness especially in hott concernements hott women hott pottage and angry tupps be ware of and pray to be delivered from.

-13. tuesday.

Att night I went to John Hasleden into Haydocke he had a letter come from London and he went to gett workman to come and helpe him it was a very rainy night and filthy gate and very darke.

-15. thursday.

Att night old Ezibell envited John Haselden dicke Asmull and I to drinke with her son in law we went in night but before we went I was somewhat disconsulate and was in shop and Mary Naylor came into shop and we stayd togather and it did satisfie me very much. She would have me to bringe her Mr which I did. Afterwards when I had taken a leave of her I went with some young folkes to this mans house and by vertue or Mayres compaine it made me as hearty as might be.

-16. friday.

I was sent for to Thomas Heyes I went when I came thither it was but upon shop affaires. I set forward to Banfer longs there I stayd and dranke Botle Ale and common ale and was very merry. Set forward for hime when I was about Rogr Naylors I went in and Mary was angry with me I had beene out of shop for folkes had beene there enquiring for me which angered her very sore soe she was troubled att me.

-17. Saturday.

I had a very sickly day but the lord instigated the pain my love was very earnest to Mary att this time. This night was a sad night to me in paine of my head but the Lord was favourable to me in the morneing for I was in health. I blesse god weepeing my endure for a night but joy comes in the morneing.

-18. lords day.

I went downe to Mary when her father was come up to chappell she was very respectfull to me I was not harty this day but in a sad condition.

-19. Munday.

Ann Greinsworth came to towne to goe brew att lodge. I was glad to see her went and brought her to Ellin Ashton spent 2d on her.

-21. Wedensday.

I went to Rogr Naylors as I came againe att Thomas Naylors I bought a Henn and 6 chickens for 6d afterwards Ann Barrow sent for me to John Naylors. I went and we conferred together of time and place when and where and I must meete her. But in this discourse I intreated for myselfe to be the next in succession if in the case they two should breake of to which she did not say no neither yea when I parted I sett forward to Banfer longe where Ellin Scott did joyfully enteritaine me. After I had gotten refreshments I came home.

-22. Thursday.

Roger Naylor and Thomas Unsworth came to towne to me and envited me to ale house and Rogr said it should cost me mnothinge soe I went and when we ware togethr we ware discourseing of Esops fables. I was speaking of the fable of dogge and peece of flesh who swimming over river caught shadow and lost substance. Says Rogr take [care] of you doeing so which speech did much amaze me for I was troubled att it very sore bit I made my prayr to the lord andthe lord relieved he is my shepherd he will provide therefore I fear not. This night James Low and I went together to Banfer longe and stayed there till far in the night there was Ann Marsh there who he wood and Ellin Scott and I talked of other things. I had a great cold that troubled me very sore.

-23. friday.

Rogr Naylor went from home and I went to house amd Mary and I sat togather in parlor and it satisfied me very much.

-25. lords day.

Ann Barrow came to Ashton and gave me a lettr to answer for her into Yorkeshire to Richard Naylor. This evening olf Izibell and John Haselden and I went to Gawthers and ware merry when we pted we went all together into old John Jenkins we thought he would have dyed this night when I was with him he shooke me by the hand and I conferred with him after awhile I parted.

-27.

My Mr came to towne and was very loveing to me wished me to get all the monys I could against Christmas. Henry Low came to town and would hve me speake to Elizabeth Hindley for him wh I promised to doe this evening. I went with James Naylor into Golborne a wooing to Ann Barrowe I was at this time very sad in spirit for I had not seen Mary of a good while.

-28. Wednesday.

Mary Naylor went to Warrington and stayd all night att her unkle John Lowes in Boome and upon the ...

-29. Thursday.

I went as far as two Neawton to meet her but I could not light of her and came home againe in a sadd fitt, this night John Haselden and I went to Banfer longe and ware very wellcomly entertained and as we came home we talked of wenches. He told me that he loved a wench in Ireland att this time I did love Mary extreamely and was sad I could not see her notwithstanding.

-30. friday.

She came to me and was very loveing which did very much satisfie me.

-31.

My brothers wife came and brought me nuts and victualinge. This night I went up Greene to Mary but could not have the oportunite to speake to her.

November 1663.

-i. lords day.

Mr. Woods came to towne he was att William Haselden att dinner. I went to bring himme a pipe of tob but could not stay for I was ingaged into Compenie Ann Barrow and James Naylor and we ware all togeather at noone in Gawthrs Mr. Woods left word with Izabell that he would go to Robt Rosbotham to be all night and would hve me to come to hime so att night Thomas Smith and I went thithr but we went away by Petr Lealands Thomas sent me into house and stayd for me. When I came to door they were singing psalmes I went in and Petr would have me pray but I was unfitt at that time and so desird excuse wenches (?) and went altogather to Robt Rosbotham. Thos Smith and I ware altogather and he spoke low and told us to be intended a communion thursday night next at James Lowes Neawton Comin.

-2. Munday.

I went downe to Rogr Naylors and Mary was not so favourable to me as I conceived she should be and I was troubled very sore.

-3. Tusday.

It was Ashton Court and I was to sue John Robbinson he had given his word for Robbin Taylor it was a great trouble to my spirit. My Brother came to me this night and was all night with me I was up till far in the night to hear vaudict.

-5. Thursday.

att night I went to James Lowes of Neawton longe there Mr Woods was and a company of Christians where we received comunion and Mr. Woods preacht out of 7 Ecclesiastes 14 verse. Mr. Gregg was at prayr when I came in it was a joyfull night and sad night.

Mr. Thomas Gregg, who is several times mentioned in the diary, was minister of St.Helens, and was allowed to keep his chapel without conforming. He is described as a very courageous man, 'preaching mostly in the chapel, or openly in houses, in the face of danger, and yet was never imprisoned.' His name is found attached to the humble address and petition (of the ministers of the Gospel in the county palatine of Lancaster) to the King, December, 1660.

-7. Saturday.

Att night I went with Thomas Rosbotham James Lee James Naylor and foomert huntinge but we catched a hedge hogge but nothing els.

-8. lords day.

att night Richard Weinwright came to me and said he would go to Banfer longe. I said I would goe with hime if he would let me ride behind hime which he promised to do anon Ellin Scott came riding from Holland and her mother was on foote waiteing att Rogr Naylors. When we mett these I would have turnd home againe but they would not lett me but set me behind old woman on horseback so we rid like Irish folkes. When we came there we spent night in feasting and discoursing and att 10 of the Clocke in night dick and I tooke horse and parted.

-9. Monday night.

I went with James Naylor to old Barrowes in Golborne to woo Ann it was very dark and stormy and late in night ere we came home.

-12.

Graye Garard had an Ale cald neighbors went to spend money I went and spent ... and I came hime to bed and left neighbours and musicke and all.

-13. friday.

Jane Wright Mr. Sorowcolds maid came to towne and we ware very merry togathr I accommodated her with ale and so we parted. I was att this time in a very faire way for pleasing my carnell selfe for I knew my selfe exceptable with Emma Pottr notwithstanding my love was entire to Mary Naylor in respect of my vow to her and I was in hopes that he fathr countenanced me in the thinge.

> In the Manchester Courier notes on the diary, 'J.E.B.' observes with reference to the numerous passages about 'accommodating' one another with ale, some (particularly teetotallers) may see in the custom more than is really implied by it. The morning draft at the ale-house was merely the draft that accompanied the first meal, and is almost equivalent to ou word 'Breakfast.' Jeaffersons, in the 'Book About the Table,' cautions readers of old biographies not to attribute tavern-hunting propensaties to sober and discrete gentlemen, who, though they always opened the day with drink and gossip at an ale-house, were no wastrels or ill livers (vol. 1 p.219).

-15. lords day.

it was a very rainy day and Mr. Blakeburne came out to Chappell but sent Mr. Barkon(?) to read and I was somewhat troubled old Rogr Naylor came and sate with me all afternoone. This day was not well spent I must confesse the lord humble me for it.

The names Mr Blackburn and Mr. Barker are not given in Baines' lists of the local nonconforming ministers. Mr. Barker, Bowker, or Barkon, of Winwick, or Standish must be added to the list of the Puritian clergy of Lancashire on the authourity of Roger Lowe's Diary.

-16.

I kept shop all day and had a fire old Rogr Naylor came to me and Thomas Smith and we spent each of us 1d. for Ale. I was heartless att the prsant.

-18. Wedensday.

I was sent for to Banfore longe and called at Thomas Heyes and received 8s for comodities then went to Banfur longe where I was accomodated with ale and when I had writt some accounts for Anne I pted and came to Rogr Naylors where Mary was busy. I had a deals to say to Mary but could not have the opertunitie soe came to shop.

-20. friday.

I was ent for to Banfer longe to Ann Greinsworth to write a letter to London to her brother and I went.

-22. lords day.

I went to Leigh and cald of Ann Barrow and shee tooke me into the parlor and gave me spiced beere and we confered awhile. I spoke much for myselfe by way of motive that she would expect of me and after awhile pted being enjoined by her to come at noone backe again. I went to Leigh and att noone John and I went to Twisse barne to see all those preparations in readinges to the casting of Leigh great Bell and third bell both which bells lay in steeple. We came up to Richard Darwell and spent 2d and came into towne and so pted I sat forward for home and by the way cald on Ann Barrowe according to promise but she was sent for to go and into Pemberton but she left word I must stay till she came but I would not but Elizabeth Hart told me that shee said that if she thought her fathr would dye soone he would waite for me bec' I had presented me effections to her and this shee said upon bettr motive to see her for me - but yet the greefe of all was behind for Bett told me how pfidiously and knavish James Naylor had dealt with me for he wooing Ann would allwayes have me with hime and I had some effections to his sister and had spent her severall little notes which shee putt in a box and this one eveninge the 9 h of this prsant Novembr and he called for a band and Mary bid hime go take one out of her box so he rifled her box up and tooke all my lettrs which I had sent her att seaverall occasions and tooke them in his pockett and when we came into Goleborne to Barowes I went into parlor to John Hart and he followed Ann into anothr chamber and let her see my sacrets to Mary and I had witt in one that I wished Mary would be as faithfull to me as Ann was to him and this this stinkinge Rascall betrayed his one sister and me who I allwayes with and spent monys for his sake and advised hime the best I could nay and above all he backebit me and said it would doe well if I could get monys against my comeing out and said I durst never come in his fathers sight which was lye he said as soone as his sistr angred hime he would tell his father of all and this the actinge of a seeminge prtende friend to me as can be when in truth is no better than a deivelish malacious disembling knavish rascall but Ann was displeased att me att first tho caryd nobly and loveingly to my face but bett Hart told me this might know my friends know my foes and now its best to gett and feare god for a friend for wee see man will faile us and world will fail us but god will not faile those that trust in hime but this was matter of much greife to me and I was very sad upon it. I tooke leave from Bett and cald att old James Bammes. John his sonne did manifest abundance of love to me gave me aples brought me to Edge greene made me to promise to come att Christmas. So that the lord will not leave me friendless in this world.

The entry respecting the casting of Leigh Bells is particularly interesting, and the locality of Twiss Barn may be readily surmised from the survival of the name in Twist-lane. The bells seen by Roger Lowe are not those now in the church tower. In 1740 six bells - the third to the eighth - were placed in the tower, the eighth bell bearing the inscription - 'Willm Farrington, Vicar; John Heyes, chwarden. We were all cast at Gloucester by Abel Rudhall. 1740.' The first and second bells of the present peal were added in 1761, and the priest's bell in 1755.

-23.tusday.

I went to Rogr Naylors he was gone to Chester and I told Mary all above writt and all of James knaverie to me and her and she was highly offended and was very respectful to me att night she sent for me, James would have me be all night with hime, and she told me what she had said. I did not stay all night but came to shop to injoy bed and as I was comeing I mett with Richard Mowell of Warrington apothecarie and John Earle who tooke me with them to Ale-house.

-25 tusday.

I kept shopp all day onely Ann Barrow and her sister came to go to Petr Kenions and I brought Ann towards that place and spoke my mind to her concerning James fast against me. I was very much displeased concerning it when I came to shop I was sad all day after but God is my comfort and tho I walke in greefes yea in the vale of death yet then gods rod and staffe will be matter of comfort to me.

i December 1663.

-tusady.

Being Warrington faire I kept shop all day being very solemne and sad. Henry Low came and we discoursed togathr about our effaires and greefes. I went with him to bottome of towne field and there parted with a joint resolution that what we said each to other should lye dead. This night Richard Naylor came to me wished me to come down to his fathers house which I did. He was very sad concerninge Elizabeth Seddon acteings to him wished me to compose a lettr to her in his name which I did.

-6. lords day.

I went to Leigh John Chadockes wife was brought to Bed att noone. I parted with Leigh and came towards home and cald att Henry Barrow in Goleborne but Ann Barrow was gone from home so I came forward to Rogr Naylor and stayd supper Rogr forced me to stay. I was very glad to see that respect I see I had from them.

From the Lancashire Visitation of 1664 it appears that John Chaddock of Chaddock county of Lancaster who died c.1634, married Emma, daughter of John Potter, of Ashton county of Lancaster and had issue John Chaddock. who died unmarried and Thos Chaddock of Chaddock. The latter died c.1644 leaving by his wife, Jane, daughter of Richard Tonge of Tonge county of Lancaster, to sons, Thomas Chaddock of Chaddock aged 24, in September, 1664, and John Chaddock of Leigh aged 22, and then married to Mary daughter of William Tipping of Irlam county of Lancaster. The younger son was probably the one referred to in the diary.

-9. Wedensday.

I went to Banfer longe was very much made of tooke leave and came to Thomas Heyes and stayd awhile and then came home.

-11. friday.

att night Henry Lowe came to me to goe with hime a wooinge to Thomas Heyes to Ann Haselden she tented her sister who was lyeing in and Ann had removed me sundry times to get Henry to come and this night we both went and had spiced drink and very much made we ware but it was a very darke night and we stood without great while ...

[Two pages gone from the diary.]

January 1633-4.

-Saturday.

being envited and leave granted by my Mr to goe to Hughes Hindley of Westleigh this day I went with John Hasleden and ware all night and other day we went to Leigh and then to Hughes after dinner went forward to Ashton.

Februery 1633-4.

-1. Sabath Day.

att night I went to Mr. Woods and we being some younge people yt sometimes associated togather and providence seeming to make breach amongst us we ware sore discomforted some in their removeall far of and I myself in thoughts of being removed out of towne.

-2. Munday.

we went again viz Thomas Smith and I being envited to have spent the night to the edifaction of one another. Att this time I was sore discouraged in regard John Chadocke my fellow aprntice was in goeing from my Mr and knew not how God would dispose for me but the lord is my trust and in God is my confidence.

-5. Thursday.

before day my fellow aprntice John Chadocke cald me up with Will Parkinson John Hindley and others he was goeing to be married and had stolne his love away from Mr Whiteheads and my Mr. gave his assent I should goe with them. I gate a horse of Will Sixsmith and we went together to Billing chappell and stayd att Humphrey Cowleys till 2 came againe from fetching Mr Bispham when they brought word they must meet att Holland at once Thomas Prescott. We took horse came thithr got the ceronomie overpast and dined. I was sent afore to Wiggan to buy 7 yards ribbon and they came to Wiggan we each of us had a yard of ribbon of 12d p yard and so rid through towne. I saw them through towne and so pted I was all this while in a sad heart.

> The John Chaddock, who was Lowe" fellow-apprentice, and to whose elopement the diarist refers, it is clear could not have been the John Chaddock mentioned in the entry for the 6th. of December, 1663, but probally a namesake. The 'Mr. Bispham,' who officiated at this wedding may probally be identified with William Bispham, M.A., who was presented in May 22, 1628 to Lymm Church, and was afterwards Prebentary of Chester, rector of Eccleston, county of Chester and also Brindle, county of Lancaster. Walker states that he was ejected in 1642 but restored 1662. He was not, however, restored to the living in Lymm. He died in 1685, aged 80. It is possible, however, that the Mr. Bispham of the diary, was then residing near Wigan, may have been a relation only of the Rev. Wm. Bispham.

-13. friday.

Thomas Smith came to me to goe to ... att Mr. Woods I went and Mr. Woods and I sat till far of night talking about ministers and other things. He said Mr. Callamy who was put in prison for preaching one Sabath day had above 500li given him in one weekes imprisonment of his beloved people.

-15. lords day.

I went to Leigh and as sonn as I came there my Mr and dame both said I must have measurd taken for me a suite of clothes and a cote and Tayor came att night to take measure of me but my Mr would let me have nothinge but a cote soe I would have none and parted with greefe and as I came I overtooke Hugh Hindley and I told him my greefe. He bid me feare not he would goe to him the other day and would move him but the consideration of this moved me to greater lamentaion. In my comeing home at noone Robt Reynolds tooke me into George Norris and wee 2 with Clarke were merry awhile and then parted afterward we went into Robert ffeildings and ware with Thomas Naylor and he would not let me pay nothinge soe we parted and went to church.

-17. Tusday.

I went to Leigh very early and soe I tooke John Chadocke in bed he opened shop door and he went to bed againe. I satt att beds feete and we talked of every thinge somethinge about his marriage and about what had hapned upon Lords day about clothes for me and att this time I expected some angr from my Mr but he said nothing to me but John told me my dame was displeased that I should be so hasty nevertheless amidst all this my trust is in the Lord.

-18. Wednesday.

Widow Lowe came and gave me 1s. for sermon writinge.

Roger Lowe appears to have had plenty of opportunities of earning money in his spare moments by making writings for his neighbours, such as letters, wills, amd official documents. This above entry affords evidence of the wide spread practice of taking notes of the heads of sermons, and it appears to have benn Roger's custom to report, for his own and friend's edifacation, the discources he heard in chapel or church.

-22.

Thos Smith and I went to Mr Woods and ware [there] all night Mr. woods was gone to the funerall of his wives mother soe I repeated sermon there was foure young folkes prsant [who] stayd on purpose to hear repetition.

-28. saturday.

Tho Smith and I went to Robert Rosbotham in Parke lane being very welcomly entertained. Our discourse was about these times and the other morning being lords day I was expected to pray and after we had had prayer and a ch.. and resolve with other things we came towards Ashton chappell being envited to come again but this time I was very sad in consideration .. providence towards me .... the greatr will in time not deny the lesse and why should I fear. Gods providence is the poor mans inheritence and God hath enough in store for me for the earth is the lords with the fullness thereof therefore its good to wait and trust in the Lord.

-10. Wedensday.

I went to Thomas Heyes and Bafer longe to reckon and at this time Ann Greensworth was pswaded I loved Ellin Scott and I satisfied her to the contarie. I writ her some lettrs and so parted.
-14.

att evening prayr I went to Alehouse with one Rogr Lowe and spent 4d. but had a very sickle night and .....

-15. Munday.

I had avery sad sickly day all day but the lord strengthed me.

-19. friday.

I cast up debt booke and see how I stood with my Mr and my charge was to my Mr that I had in goods for my Mr 148li 8s. 9d. in one year and his receit in mony from me and in debts 135li 5s. 1d. and this did rejoice my spirit.

-21. lords day.

I went to Leigh ans stayd till noone and Mr. James Woods was there and envited me to his house all night. I went to hime to Georg Norris house att after dinner and spent 3d so parted thence I went to see my sister Katherin gave her 4d so came to my Mr and parted and intended to Hugh Hindleys for John Hasleden was there and I was to come to him but I ... Hugh and family towards church and John was gone for Ashton so I parted and came my selfe and cald on my sister Ellin and so parted and as I was comeinge near Barrowes Ann Barrow cald for me for we had been out one against the other so I went to her shee tooke me into the parlor and we rectified all businesses and so I came away.

-25. thursday.

Thomas Atherton was to part with neighbours so I was envited amongst neighbours to go to alehouse to drinke and John Pottr and I began to discourse concerning the manner of God's worship he was for Episcopacie and I for Presbittery. The contention had like to have beene hott but the lord prvented. It was 2 or 3 dayes ere we speake and I was afraid lest he should doe me some hurt and I went into house and all angr was removed.

The diarist's intercourse with the ejected Presbyterian ministers and his education under the influence of Puritanism appear from any entries to have engendered a love of religious contoversy. The record of the contention with John Potter is in point, and either intentionally or as a consequence of careless spelling, the entry contains a happy reference to Presbyterian sternness where he declares that he stood up against his friends and befended 'Presbittery.'

March 1663-4.

-6. day lords day.

I was very pensive an sad all day and I betooke myself to solitarines for I walked down to town heath and I presented my suplication to the lord I prayed to God and showed all my touble and I hope the lord heard for I was abundantly comforted in my spirit.

-8. tusday.

John Hasleden James Jenkins and I walked into fields, John Hasleden had ingaged himselfe to Dicke Asmall night before in a drunken humour to serve him as aprentice for 4 yeares and we contrived how to gett him of in the feilds, This night I was in a troubled condition for Sarah Hasleden spoke in a backebiting way of me and she would tell her brother of me but all was in a causles mattr for me spending 2d but she was handsomely taken up in my behalf by John Pottr of lilly lane and by her husband and god onely is my defence.

-10. thursday.

Humphrey Harrison came to shop and stayd with me a great while and att last moved me to instruct his son in teachinge hime to endite lettrs and to cast account up which I promised I would doe. This night I was envited to goe to Gawhr Taylors to drinke... for wife bought her comodities for me and he said if I would not come then farewell so I was constrained to goe but I stayd but for a short time.

-11. friday.

Ann Barrow came to towne and moved me to write a lettr for her in answr to a love lettr from Richard Naylor. I did and moved her to sett her owne name. Mr. Maddocke and old Rogr ware in shop and ware very earnest to see lettr but I would not let them. Mr Maddocke and Rogr Naylor wished me to goe to alehouse with them which I did and after Mr Maddocke went with Roger home to be all night and they stayd on me till I had shutt up shop and I went down to Rogers with them and stayd supper and prayr and so came to bed.

This Mr. Maddock may have been the minister of Ashton, the successor to the Rev. James Wood on the removal of the latter from the living. An anecdote is told of an old woman, who had heard Mr. Wood's successor on the Sunday after the ejection, and remarked that if Mr. Wood had gone into the pulpit and shook his grey beard, 'it would have done us more good.'

-12. Saturday.

Mr Maddocke came with Roger Naylor and envited me to alehouse and as we ware drinking James Astley a Wiggan man came into house and gave me a letter with a lemmon which was a token sent from Richard Naylor from Wakefield Yorkshire. This night I promised to goe to Roberts Rosbothome's house and did with Thomas Smith with me and was all night and they lent me Mr. Gees booke concerninge prayr he was minister at eccleston one upon the ...

-15 day. tusday.

        I was reading in his booke and in consideration of the mans person and gravitie I was posesd with sadness and composed these verses:-
Renwned Gee thou now enjoyst glory
Yet thy name shall remaine earths lasting story
In thought of thee ah I can sitt and weepe
Yt thou by death shouldst now be laid asleepe
How lovely was thy life joyfull thy death
Angels received thy soul att latest breath
He say no more but weepe yet joy to see
Myself in hapines with blessed Gee
Gee now in joy triumhs his sorrows past
And he yt place enjoyes that aye shall last
Therefore blest Gee this once Ile bid farewell
Hopeing ere longe to be there where thou dost dwell

sic cantat
Rogerus Lowe.

His name was Edward Gee minister of Eccleston Church he dyed about or in the year 1660 or 1659 or thereabouts but the church of god sustained great lossse in his death and Mr Herles of Winwicke and Mr Johnsons of Hallgate who all flourished about this time and dyed about this time foresaid in so much as it was the lamentation of Mr Colebourne att Leigh exercises in his prayr that we now wanted our Herles our Gees and our Johnsons. This was upon the 25 decembr 1660. Old Mr Woods joined with hime.

    'J.E.B.' in the Manchester Courier notes says;- Edward Gee, the son of a Lancashire man of that name who was beneficed in Devonshire, was a native of Banbury. He was educated at Newton School Lancashire and Brasenose College and was afterwards appointed to some benefice in Lancashire (a curacy at Winwick, as appears in Beamont's History of that Parish) and made chaplin to Dr Parr, Bishop of Sodor and Man, to whose living of Eccleston, near Chorley, Gee succeeded in 1646. He may had derived much os his religious zeal from his birthplace. The associate of Herle he became a a strict and unyeilding Presbyterian. He took an active part in the establishment of that government in Lancashire, aciting for a short time as 'Scribe' or secretary to the Manchester Presbytery. In 1648, as 'Minister to the Gospel at Eccleston' he signed the 'Harmonious Consent' of the Lancashire Ministers. he is called by Martindale 'a great knocker of Disputation.' For two years Nathanael Heywood was an attendant upon Gee's ministry; but Gee was not present at his ordination. Gee was the author of some other works. One of these, 'A Treatise of Prayer"' 1653, 8vo., a book of rareity, is that to which Roger Lowe refers. He died 26th. May, 1660 and was buried in his Parish Church of Eccleston.

-17. Thursday.

My sister Ellin came to towne of Ashton to buy comodities of me. I brought her to towne Heath. I moved att partinge to serve god and go to church and labour to instruct her children in the wayes of god and in so doeinge God would blesse her and make them comfortable to her. I was att this time sad in spirit but God will refresh.

-18. friday.

I was sent for to John Naylors wife of Edge greene and I was in some greefe by reason of Cookes wife a very wrathfull malacious woman had reported that I said such things concerneing women naturall infirmities which I never did and troubled me extremely but the lord will prevent all feares and will procure respect for me.

-20. lords day.

Lidia Scott and Joseph Scott and Ralph Bradshaw came out of Dalton beyond Holland and Lidia came to me to have me to goe with them into Tankr feild. I did and att night I went to bringe them towards home and soe parted.

-21. Munday morning.

Sarah Hasleden sent me to come write a lettr for her to London which I did. This day John Haselden came into shop and James Jenkins and I said I had a brasse shillinge oh says John Haselden I have another come says he lets goe to Sar..ing Batys we can get then of. It was concluded one and we all went and when it came to the effect of the busines John 12d she received but mine she would not and they ware both in the hands of James Jenkins to give her so John Haselden bid us goe he thought he could move her to take it on or absence but it would not be. James and I waited for Johns companie home but he came not we resolved for home and when we came home we got supr. John still came not I was ill troubled that we left hime. We resolved aftr supr to sett thithr and went so we met hime in the way and came togathr into town and went to John Jenkins and there spent each 2d and ware merry in consideration of our actings.

-22. tusday.

I was sadly sicke and had a very sicke night but the lord restord me in the other morneinge.

-25. friday.

John Naylor's wife came to town and wish me to goe with her to Alehouse. I went.

-27. lords day.

Ann Greinsworth came to towne and wishd to say nothing and she would let me see a business and she pulls out a love lettr writt in Roman hand with R L in the conclusion and this was found before goles att Bankor longe directed to Ellin

33

Scott. I was something displeased but the matter was of small vallue. This day John Grimsheyes prentice came and borrowed of me 3s. 6d. and so ran away from his Mr. He borrowed it in his masters name and his master lived in Gollbourne.

Aprill 1664.

-i. Friday.

   I was sorely troubled in my mind for I had given Rogr Naylor senior great occasion of offence in telling hime of a lettr being found writt in my name and the occasion being as I supposd and I pticulerised the busines as if he should be the man and he ws highly offended att me which was my great greefe but god will help.

-2. Saturday

   John Hasleden and I went into his Brothers ground to see Colepits and this afternoone Thomas Smith and I went to Thelwall to Mr. Woods and stayd till Munday and as soon as we came thithr after a short rest we went to Grapenhall church to visit George Clare who lay sicke and I went into the church yard to look at graves as it is my comon custome and there stayed awhile admiringe the common frailtie of mankind how silently now they were lyeinge in dust. It being somewhat late we parted to Mr. Woods the next day.

- Lords day.

   We went to Limme Thomas and I and heard one Mr Grimshey out of the 36 psalme 8 verse. Att noone we came home and stayd to hear Mr. Swetnam att Thelwall out 1 James 12.

-4. Munday.

   We sett from Ashton and att Latchford Heath we mett Rogr Naylor and Petr Aspinwoll att a little Alehouse we went to them. I spent 2d with them and soe parted to Warrington where I called att Mr. Schofield shop and John Naylor and he ware togeather. He sent for Ale for me. We discoursed awhile and then parted went to Stationrs shop and Thomas Peake shop and so bid farewell to Towne came to Ashton and seaverall had enquired for me.

-5. tusday.

   I writt to Richard Naylor in Wakefield Yorkeshire.

-7. friday.

   My dame sent me 4 new bands which pleased me wery well. This night old Petr Lealand came to sit in shop a good while and att night I went to bringe hime towards home and we talked of times and about Mr. Woods after a while we parted.

-9. Eastr day.

I went to Leigh and att noone John Chadockes and I went to Lately Comon to a house cald Sumnors to se Ann Smith who was there in Hold that had drowned her child in Hurst ground and she was very much greeved as she seemed she sate at chimneys end hangeing downe her head and I spoke to her to repent told her God was mercifull he pardoned David who was adulterer and murderer. I came away being full of sorrow for her came to Leigh Church and was at his sermon. Mr. Woods maid would have gone home with hime but I refused.

Some local names in Bedford township are proved by this entry to date from at least the seventeenth century.

-11. Munday.

I was pensive and sad and went into towne feild and prayd to the Lord and I hope the lord heard.

-12. tusday.

Thomas Naylor sent for me to make bond betweene hime and Mr. Byrome. I did he gave me 6d and the neighbourhood of Ashton envited me to goe with then to Ale house this eveninge which I did spent 6d.

The Byroms of Parr Hall, in the Parish of Prescott, are referred to in Byrom's 'Remains', vol. i 614. The house called and ancient seat of the Byroms of Byrom. (See Baines, Old Ed., Vol iii 713)

-13. Wednesday.

Ellin Scott came to town and Rogr Naylor did woo her and there was some difference between hime and me and now he sent for me and this eveninge all was in love and I was glad. We see god can make then who sometimes enemies turne to be friends.

-15. friday.

I was envited to goe with Ann Taylor and Elizabeth Taylor to William Andrton in Pemberton and there was with us John Haselden Emma Pottr and others. We stayd till after sunn goeing downe and then parted came to Goose Greene and there stayd in an Alehouse but it was my great trouble to stay or to have gone this gate onely they ware good customers to me and I durst not but goe for fear of displeasure.

-17. lords day.

I began to write sermon the morneinge. John Pottr and his wife and John Haseleden in vited to efright me in telling me I was cited to Bishops court for ninconformitie to Comon Prayr so att noone John Haselden and I came together at dinner and he seluted me with this that I was cited att the hearing of which I eate no more but went to Town Heath and prayd to God to deliver me and consulted with myself how to doe but att noone it was found out and I was glad.

-18. Munday.

I writt a letter by the advice of Peter Asmull to John Haselden from his unkle from Reinford for John Speedie comeing to Reinford and I sent lettr down town by a stranger and upon the other day being tusday John hasted for Reinford away he hasted this day. See Bowden Steward att Lodge and Rogr Naylor and I ware together. John Jenkins and Old Mr. Woods came to shoppe and thought much I was in Ale warned me to take heed I told him I could not trade if it some times I did not spend 2d.

-20. Wednesday.

John Jenkins constable tooke John Haselden and myselfe to every Alehouse with hime in night in answr to warrent to make pri... search.

The search may be made by the Ashton constable may have been the customary periodical inspection in order to prepare the presentiment made by all petty constables at the County Assizes. It is possible, however, that some evil doer was 'wanted' and Constable Jenkins was armed with a special warrent to seek for him; but if so it is very likely the diarist would have mentioned it.

-24. Lords day.

I went to Leigh and I cald on my sister Ellin they gave me a cock chicken when I came to Leigh young Mr. Woods wife did very ernestly envite me home with her att noone. John Chadocke and I went into feilds and in a feild called horse shoo we sat us downe by a great pitt side and conversed togather of out greefes cencerning our calling and att night he brought me to West Leigh and our discourse was ye same.

-27. Wedensday.

Younge John Jenkinson and I went to looke Bird nests out in fields and my legs were cruely pricked. I was att this time in great fear because shopp was to be cast up and I was efraid it would not answer my Mr expectation. Now the lord help me through my prenticeship that I may be freed from these sad charges of goods I stand indebted with and are so possesed with such feares by reason on my ingagements to my Mr. I know not how to rest the lord keape me from miscaryinge for the lords sake.

May 1664.

-1. Lord's day.

I was somewhat pensive all day in consideration of my unsettlemts in this world yet much comferted in trusting in God. Men not so happy as have these wordly enjoyments as those who have god for their lord. Ann Greinsworth very earnestly envited me to Banfer longe and I promised to come.

-3. tuesday.

Henry Feildinge an Hour glasse makr whom I had hour glasses of came and I was ingaged for 1 dozen and a half of hour glasses and this day I prayd hime made meet with hime and ...

-4th May

being Wedensday I tooke 30 glasses more and he intended for Leigh and I writt a lettr to John Chadocke to move him to take some of hime and a very honest man he was to me. I had them of the rate of 10s. a dozen and sold them after 12 and he gave me 4 half hour glasses and 6d in monys when I payd hime.

-6. friday.

John Chaddocke came from Leigh to cast up shop and efraid I was least I should not answr my Mr expectation att after we had cast up shop we went to Heath a shootenge came to towne againe and supt att younge John Jenkins and was there all night. I slept litle expecting to go to Leigh the other morneinge which I did betimes in the morneinge John and I together. When we came to Leigh I was ingaged to my Mr 200li and upwards and it pleased God to blesse my indeavours that I had profited my Mr 21li 1s 5d. I was glad then I boldly spake my greevences and my Mr told me he had bought me a steake and would give me ... of it. I had measure taken for me for a new dublett and was to have a new hatt and a new pr stockings and my Mr told me he intended shop for me and att Michaelmas next I was to goe with home to Chestr faire and thus the lord favoured me and turned my feares into joyes praise the Lord O my soule.

-8th. lords day.

This evening Richard Bordman was very ill. I made his will this night.

-9th. Munday.

I went with Richard Weinwright to Nicholas Bursco marle pitt gave marlers a quarter....

-10th. tusday.

I went to Banfer longe to Ann Greinsworth but stayd not.

-11. wedensday.

I went downe to Rogr Naylors he was from home and I spoke Roughley to Mary and shee seemed to be very effectionate but I litle matered it I cald her a false dissemblinge harted person she tooke it leasurely.

-12. thursday.

Lawrance Pendlebery was maried this day and he intreated my company I desired excuse but this eveninge I went and spent 6d with them and partd.

-14th. Saturday.

I went with my brothers into Windle and upon 15th being lord's day Tho. Smith came to me and we went 2 and 2 together to Cowley Hill to hear Mr. Gregg preach att one Mrs. Harprs in the parlor. There he preached out 3 Mallachy 15. 16. 17. 18. verses. When sermon was done we came to my brothers I was not well but departed from my brothers sicke but the lord suported me that ere I gat home I was pretty well.

-17. tusday.

Ann Greinsworth sent for me to Banfer longe I writt a lettr for her to her brothers then in London she made much of me I sat downe all her accounts att this time I came away by Rogr Naylors and spoke my mind to Mary Naylor which was not expected tho was very favourable to me and I set het light as she did to me and so I parted.

-19. thursday.

I went to Billinge Chappell to a race and James Darbishire saw me and envited me to goe with him into Humphrey Cowleys to spend 2d he being from Bosson so I went and in the spence of 2d Niceolas Houghton came to as we ware in Britteine and he begun to give disdaininge words out against the art of a grocer or mercer and so pticularizd it as to me in so much as I was very angry in so much as Humphrey Cowleys wife was angry att me in a very furious manner and I was sadly troubled yet the wife went out and some compeny as she went out too comended me highly in so much as she came againe and made a recantation for what she had said and I was bettr satisfied.

-20. friday.

John Jenkinson and Joshua Naylor and I went to gathr to take a threstoll nest by chance we mett with a py annot nest we tooke [it] every one had one pye and one we gave to Tho. Winstanly and so came home. Old Jenkins this day came and payd me for making his will and otr things he payd me 11s 9d. tooke me to ale house and spent 6d on me this night. John Jenkins constable and I went to gathr to lay night hookes but

-21.

goeing there nothing was found.

-22. lords day.

I went to Wiggan and heard Mr Thomas Blakeburne preached I dined at Thos Leighs John Jenkins and wife preached were both with me.

-24. tusday.

John Naylors wife sent for me to writ a lettr for her to one Mrs Shaw in Neston in Worrall in Cheshire and I went and she made much of me.
-28.

this morneinge I went be time to Leigh and was pretty hearty in my returne.

-30th. Munday

I went to Billinge and bought tenn dozen of styth stones for to send to Leigh I was in pensive condition at this time.

June 1664.

-4. Saturday.

Gilbert Naylor came to me to have me to goe with him to his sister Margaretts into Houghton. I went with hime this eveninge and att Castke Hill in Hindley he would have me to goe into Astleys an alehouse and as we were drinkinge Robbert Reynolds junior of Leigh but now of Blackerhead came in he was now sett up at Balckerhead he was glad to see me. We satyd drinkinge of 8d and I paid not a 1d so we parted and came to Houghton Common and went into William Reynolds house and William discoursed and told us many things concerninge Dean Church Mr. Tilsley and Mr. Eangr who being a conformer. We partdd from then and went to Hugh Rigbie that was ye place we intended too and they ware in bed wife gets up makes fire gets us suppr and we go to bed with an intention to go to Deane Church in the morninge but we lay too longe in or beds. After dinner we sett towards home which I came to Ashton Mary Naylor had a sweetheart comne and I was somewhat greeved and went to Towne Heath and meditated upon these words its good to hope and quietly waite. Obs. yt hopeing and waiting for a possible thing is a Ctian duty in time of difficultie.

Mr John Tinsley, M.A. of Glasgow University was the minister of Dean Church. He was an active member of the Second (Bolton) classis. In 1647-8 he is described in the Manchester parish registers as 'minister of the Word of God at Deane Church but living in Manchester.' Bishop Wilkins after the Bartholomew Act, allowed him to hold a lecturer's place in the church; but he suffered ejectment under the two other bishops. He died in Manchester, 1684 and was buried at Deane 16th. Dec. Mr John Angier, who is probally refered to in his entry, was minister of Denton, a venerable man who had received ordination at the hands of Dr. Lewis Bailey the author of 'The Practice of Piety' a work which is mentioned by Lowe in the diary. So much was Angier respected by the Bishop of Chester and others that he continued to hold his chapel without making any formal profession of conformity, not being, therefore, actually a conformer. His name is not found in 'The Harmonious Consent' of the Lancashire Ministers. As Moderator of the Manchester Presbytery for the time being, his name attached to the Presbyterian arguments at Mossley's 'Excomminicatio Excommunicata, 1658.' He was the author of the remark on long sermons: ÒIwould rather leave my hearers longing than loathing.'

-13 Munday.

Thomas Jameson was in Jenkins and sent for me to come to drinke with hime and we satayd late in night and we began controversie he a papist began to speak revileingly of Luther and Calvin which I laboured to defend conceininge them to be meere callummies of the papists because of his revolt from his frienship. We ware in love and peace in our discourse.

-14. tusday.

Att night Ralph Hasleden sent for me his youngest daughter was dead it was conceived she had eaten asnicke for Sarah had laid asnike in meale and in butter and the child getting it gett that which was laid in buttr and so dyd and he intreated me to go to Warrington to Mr Finches to gett them to come to funerall which I did and called at Winwicke and bespoke bread and drinke and when I came to the fomost Mrs Finch would not let me goe till the next morninge for it was late so I stayd and att day I arose and went to sadle horse and so came home.

Mr. Henry Finch was formerly of Walton, and a preacher in 'the field country' as Calamy calls the Fylde. After the ejection he retired to Warrington, where Lowe saw him. He subsequently settled at Birch Chapel, Manchester.

-15. Wedensday.

My dame came to the funerall and sent for me to come and bring all monys with me I had to pay for funerall expences with when we came to Winwicke they caused me to set down in the sellr to take account of flaggons drawen. I rid home and att Thomas Rothwells we stayd drikeinge but the

-16th day thursday.

I lay all day sike but was much comforted by Enn Potts care of me.

-20. Munday.

I went to Bamfor longe and was much made of ecquenting Ann Greinsworth of a servent maid she might have.

-21. tusday.

Matthew Low and I ware falne out a litle and he came to shop and we went to alehouse and ware reconcild.

-23. Wednesday.

I went to Leigh and gave my dame 9li in monys. She would have the Taylor take measure on me for a pair of breeches dublett and cote and she and I went into shop to look out cloth and she made me take my choice soe we tooke two remlents into house and she kept them in her custordie this newes sent me joyfullie towards Ashton. It was the Lord that moved her nay she was so forward as she wuld have had the tailor lett others worke for to have done my clothes against Sabbath day.

-26. lords day.

Edmund Winstanley envited me to dinner with hime and I went.

July 1664.

-3. lords day.

I went to Leigh I had a new suite of clothes and a coat. I went to William Gerrards and we discoursed awhile concerninge my time and other things so I parted. Att night my dame would not let me goe till I had supd. I came to Ashton and went to John Jenkins and anon Mr James Sorrowcold came into house and he spent 6d on me. I brought hime home for he tooke me alonge with hime and I was all night and I lay in his cambr.

-4. Munday.

bedtime in the morninge I came from Leigh home John Chaddock was comin from Leigh and he had some commodities of me. I brought hime agate towards home.

-4. tusday.

Very early went to Leigh.

-10. lords day.

I was envited by Widow Taylor to ride before her daughtr to the funerall of Thomas Taylor of Sankey Hall and I assented. Ralph Hasleden and his wife and Elizabeth Taylor rid altogather. This Evening I was all night at Sankey Hall there was att the Hall a young man a papist named Robert Kenion he and I conversed longe togeather about papistrie and after our discourse he was very loveinge.

-11. Munday.

Early I got up and went to Warrington and in Mr Pickerings shop I found paraton dicke Tilsley and Ale he would give me so I went with him and stayd

41

awhile and so parted. So went to Hall there was wine and bisketts to be had. So about 11 clocke he was fatched out and led on a coach to Winwicke and this is the conclusion of this story by which we may se how that one day friends and world and all here below we must part with the grave is the parting place. Friends that did much honor this funerall came to attend it to the grave and there parted. Now the lord grant us such grace as tho we may pt with friends and world yet we may never part with Christ and that will be our comfort.

-14. Thursday.
I was with Daniel Chaddocke and Dr. Naylor in the Ale house and I was very sicke.

-15. friday.
I went to Warrington to buy candles of Richard Nichols. I had but 4 dozen and I brought them upon horseback.

-17. lords day.
I went with Thomas Smith to St. Ellin Chappell and we cald on my brother and refreshed ourselves with victuals and so went to Chappell. It was a very rainy day. Mr. Ambrose preached. We came home at noone and Mr. Asmull preached in Ashton.

> This entry gives a clue to the date of the death of the Rev. Isaac Ambrose of Preston which does not appear to have been correctly recorded. The event is said to have occurred in 1663-4 whereas it must have been late in the year. In a later entry on the 28th. May, 1666, Lowe notes that upon reaching hime he read certain Psalms in metre 'in a book of Mr. Ambroses, late minister of Preston.' The death of Ambrose, who was well known throughout Lancashire, directed greater attention to his works, the pathos and beauty of which were appreciated by the late Rev. Joseph Hunter. Of these works his 'Looking into Jesus' was the most popular.

-22 friday.
I went with John Jenkinson to Wiggan and I gatt in that old debt that was oweinge me per Humphry Roubothom a pedlr in Wiggan.

-24 lords day.
I went with Tho Smith to Wiggan and we heard Bishop preach. Dined at Eles Leighes. Robert Reynolds was in towne he gave 2d in Ale to me and enjoyned me to make for hime an indenture because that Wiginrs did threaten him. I parted from him and att after Eveininge prayr Thomas and I came to Ptr Lealands and was all night. The other day comeinge home I mett with Thomas Heyes who said he had been att shop att one but found me not so he desird me to go backe with hime to William Chaddockes to make up some accounts so I did and they gave me 6d so I parted.

-28. thursday.

I was intreated p Richard Asmall to go with to goe with hime and John Hasleden into Hindley. There was a wench he had a child on hime so we went and in Mr. Lanckton fields she was and she ardently manifested hime to be the father of the child in her wombe so we pted. Att platt bridge he tooke us into Hugh Platts and spent 6d on us as I came home I cald att Banfer longe and Ann was glad to see me.

-29. Saturday.

One Mr Lowe vicar of Highton came to towne and would have me to come to hime and abundance of effection he prtended to me but att last we began in disputage about Episcopecie and prsbittrey. He said they were apostollicall. Yea both quoth I they are apostollicall from the truthes [?rites] of God and he seemed to be displeased.

August 1664.

-8. Munday.

Being Ashton wakes att this time I had most ardent effection to Emm Pottr and she was in company at Tankerfields with Henry Kenion and it greeved me very much. Henry Low came to me and would have me to go to Tankerfeilds and spend 2d so we went the next chambr to that they were in. Att last they came by us and I moved Emm to stay to drinke with me which she did but would not stay with me neither there nor nowhere else would not come to me though she said she would and I was in a very sad eflicted estate and all by reason of her.

-10. Wedensday.

Emm went to bringe one Pegg lightfoote tords home and I went after her and we spoke to each other and Ellin Harrison came unto us and tooke us and was in a great rage against Emm and this was mattr of great grief of harte unto me but my trust is on God who will helpe in trouble. Tho storme be now yet I have hopes I shall see a calm this is my hopes and till then I'll waite one god.

-14. lords day.

I went to Neawton and heard Mr. Blakeburn and he enjoyed old William Hasleden and I came to Rothwells which we did and had 2 pints of wine which he would have paid for but I would not suffer it. Aftr I came home I went to Elizabeth Rosbothom and I spoke my mind to her concerninge Emm which I could not doe with out teares and she did pitie my state I was very discomforted.

-15. Munday.

The sun began to shine for Elizabeth Rosbotham had told Ellin my greefe and she pitied my condition so as she resolved she would nevr act against me so. I went to John Rosbothams and stayed awhile and both Ellin and Emm came down and Ellin went way and Emm and I went into chambr and there we pfessed each other loves to each other soe I was abundantly satified within my selfe and I promised this night to come to see her in her chambr. God will arise and show pitie to his distressed servant.

-16.

Old Mr Woods came to town and was all night att William Haseldens and they would have had me supr but Mr. Woods ingaged me to come to be with hime. I was this after noone with Willm Chadocke and Thomas Heyes casting up their accounts and after I had done with them I came to shop and shutt it up and went to William Hasledens they ware att pryr aftr prayr Mr. Woods discourse was concerneinge wars and troubles that he and old William had beene in togather so att far in night I came me way and came to the window that Emma Pottr lay in chambr and I would gladly have come in but she durst not let me in but she rise up to the window and we kisd so I went to bed.

-17.

Att night I went to Docke-lane to get Raph Hasleden to goe for me to Leigh to fetch goods he was not att home but I spoke to Sarah and bought 2lb. of wax.

-18 Thursday.

This morneing we went with cart and watrs were at Penington bridge. We gat or commodities into cart and so parted Leigh and came well home.

-19. friday.

I borrowed a horse and went to Humphrey Burscoes in Lowton for to buy hony and wax of his sistr but they ware too hard for me.

-20. Saturday.

Constables Hadocke and Golborne came to have me write their prsentements for assizes and when I had done I writ poore is provided highwaies repaired thes queries answered and clarke unrewarded att which they laughed most heartily.

-22. Munday.

I was desired by Banther Taylor wife to ride before Eles her daughter to the funerall of Lucie Taylor of Sankey Hall and I left my Mrs occasions att Ashton to answr their expectation. Went to Sankey Hall came againe with bringinge to Winwicke and whiles drinkinge was I get Emm into a place above where we talked about some things and in this while Eles Taylor like an unworthy woman went and took another to ride before her so that when I came to take horse there was none for me I was hughly prplexed yet bore it very patiently. John Moody and I cane home togethr and as we ware comeinge John Pottr and Emm behind hime overtooke

44

us and he asked me what I would give him att Neawton I promisd hime a qt of Ale and at Neawton he light and we stayd and ware very merry. Anon dicke Naylor comes and falls a quarrellings with in so much as we fell to it but John Pottr vindicated my cause nobly and poor Emm stickd close to me so they gatt dicke away with deal of shame to his part so we all came togather home and William Sixsmith would needs have John Moody and I ride behind hime which we did and so ridd into town but it was night. I tooke John Pottr into Alehouse and spent 6d on him.

-26. friday.

   I went to docke-lane to see Ralph this morneinge who had received hurt by a fall of a horse as he was goeinge to assizes. I was very much troubled in my thoughts by reason of Dr. Naylors and mine falling out but especially my greefe was bec' of my great love for Emm which by reason of my longe time could not be perfected but god is alsufficient. Trust in the lord o my soule and thou shalt see the event of all to gods glory and they comfort in the end.

-28. lords day.

   I went to Leigh my Mr was gone to Assizes att noone I was very disconsulate but I went to John Chaddockes house and I mett with John Hindley we went hee and I to top of steeple and discoursed of formr dayes and passages past and gone. There was buryd one Sande Sixes who had his necke broken in rideinge between dean church and bent. When we ware come from top of steeple John Chadocke was seekinge us so we went altogather to ale house and spent each of us 1d so parted. Att night I came home to Ashton and went to see Ralph Hasleden and parted and came to bed.

-29. Munday.

   Dr. Naylor came to me and we were in John Jenkins and made friends and ware very merry. The lord worked graciously for me in many respects therefore I blesse the lord.

-30. tusday.

   Young Mr Woods came with his servant to go to Georg Markland and I gat a horse and went with hime. We dined at Widow Clarkes in Windle aftr I came home I went to Robert Rosbotham.

Mr. James Woods was minister at Chowbent. He was of the same spirit as his father, and suffered temporary ejectment. His marriage is recorded by Roger Lowe in June, 1663. He was followed into the pulpit by his son 'General Woods' of local history.

September 1664.

-4. lords day.

   I was with Mr Sorowoolds servants in Ale house and was merry.

-5. Munday.

I went to my father [godfather] Stirrops to buy hony and wax and I gat Ann Taylor to goe with me. My father was not att home so I bargained not.

-10. Saturday.

I was envited to go to the funerall of old Asmull at Sendelly Greene. I went with John Hasleden and John Pottr to Winwicke.

-11. lords day.

I went to Wiggan with John Pottr to hear Bishop but he was gone. We stayd all afternoone in Eles Leighes and att night we came hme and I went into Thomas Harrison and Emm had been with Kenion she told me but it was against her will.

At the time of the diarist the Rev. George Hall, Bishop of Chester, was residing in Wigan.

-12. Munday.

Mr. [Henry] Gerrard of Bain forlonge came to town and envited me to Tankerfields and gave me the ale and envited me to his house.

-16. friday.

Att night between the hours of 7 and 8 departed this life Richard Bordman in Ashton. I waked most of this night John Pottr and I went to ring bell. He dyd of dropsie.

-17.

I went to Winwicke to the interrinage of said Bordman.

The entry of the last burial of Richard Bordman is interesting as an instance of a common sanitary precaution taken by the relatives, more common in the 17th. century that at the present among the people of Lancaashire.

-18.

I went with John Pottr to Wiggan to hear Bishope.

-19.

Mr. Pottr came to towne and I made a Bond for him and Ann Johnson he recd 20li. in monys I made it in hast. Mr. Henry Gerrard came to town and caused me to goe with him to Ellin Ashton he spent his 6d on me and envited me to come to Beinfor longe.

-21. Wedensday.

Dr. Naylor met with me with a younge man with hime who intreated me to get his sistr out for that younge man soe I promised I would do my

46

endevor. I went to Thomas Naylor and get her leave to go to an Ale that had old Harvie wife had so as soone as I had her out I conferrd her upon the younge man so I went away to home and told Emm what I had done and she was very angry.

-25. lords day.

It was a very rainy morneinge and I went for to go to Leigh but was prevented by raine. I went to Chappell and at noone when I came out of it it was faire and I sett forward for Leigh and I ovrtooke John Naylor of Edg greene he would needs have me to goe drink but I as I came againe he light of me to goe supd with hime I did so and came home I delivrd to my Mr all in monys.

-25. Munday.

Tho Naylor and Thomas Greenhough came to me to make a Bond and they tooke me to Ale house and we ware merry.

-29. Thursday.

Gilbert Naylor came to have me make a bond for hime and William Sixsmith.

Octobr 1644

-2. lord's day.

I went to the funerall of old John Jenkins to Winwicke and att after drinkinge I went with John Pottr and Ralph Low church-warden to Hall Winwicke and went to see chappell and went to top of house and up and downe and then we parted and I came home and when we ware come home James Jenkins envited me and John Hasledens to go to his brothers ato spend 2d and had a business to disclose to us and none els we went and when we came it was to ecqueint us of his compeny keapeinge with a young woman who was worth 11li. per Ann in house and ground and he moved us to go with him to meet her att Warrington the lords day after and we promisd we would.

Winwicke Hall is now the rectory house attatched to the parish living, and is the residence of the Rev. Canon Hopwood, Rector of Winwicke.

-5. Wedensday.

I went to my Brothers was all night his wife was brought to bed so I was ingaged to go with him to Prescott upon lords day after. This day the Undr Sheriffe of Lancashire Mr. Robert Greinsworth came unto towne and sent for me he was friednly with me by reason I write for his mother.

-7. friday.

I went to Wiggan to have a deske made for me of James Leythest but it was not made he gave Joshua Naylor and me 6d in Ale and he would procure a wife for me Robt Winstanly daughter. John Hamson was in town and spent 4d on me or discourse was concerning his sonne to be bound to my Mr. When I came to Ashton I heard of a stirke that my Mr had sent me but it was not according to my mind I was this night with Townsmen of Ashton.

-9. lords day.

This morneing I went to mt Brothers into Windle he had a child to be christened att Prescott so I was ingaged to be the one godfather and Ralph Ralsh near Carr Mill was the othr and my coz Ann Shey was godmothr we went to Prescott and drunke att Edward Derbyshire clarke of church and Ralph Ralstr and I went to top of steeple in church. There was sexstones making grave for one Jacke or George Massy a Runr who was buryd this day att after eveninge prayr. We went to Darbishire house again and stayd and drunk it cost Ralph Ralster and me either of us 15d 2s and 6d in all and we payd it joyntly. I had intended to come home but the lateness of night prevented me so came to my brothrs and styd all night.

-16. lords day.

I went to Leigh Mr. Henwar preached at noone. John Hampson John Chadocke and I went to Jane Mulls and had discourseing about John Hampsons son who should be my Mr prentice. Att night Wiliam Knowles went home with me to Ashton as I came I over tooke sister Ellin and Mr Battersbie whome I wished to speake to my Mr concerninge me I thought it sad for me to be ingaged 9 years to stay in Ashton to sell my Mrs ware of and get no knowledge so he promised to speake to Hugh Hindley of it and they two would goe togather to my Mr and speke my greevences.

-31. Munday.

I went to Wiggan and bought 1 doz & half of twist for coates for Ralph Jenkins & stuff for a cap I ridd att this time I was somewhat troubled in my thoughts concerninge my effaires in the world. This night I was with John Pottr with his friends that ware come from Winwicke in John Jenkins I spent 10d and att far in night I went to bed.

November 1664.

-3. Wedensday.

Ellin Scott came from Beinfer longe and Richard Weniwright and I and Peter Buckstone ware all at Tankrfields takeing leave of her and we had a wessell.

Roger Lowe uses the ther '.c.wassail' ;in an incorrect sense. The right interpretation of the expression is given in 'Hamlet' (Act 1, scene iv), 'The King doth wake tonight and takes his rouse; keep wassail.'

48

-11. 12. 13. dayes.

I was in an efflicted state my body by reason of cold in so much as I could scarcely goe.

-14. Munday.

Ralph Hasleden sent for me to come to diner his child was christened the day before I went.

-20 lords day.

Thomas Smith and I went to Robert Rosbothams and stayd till far in the night & then came home.

-27. lords day.

Henry Low Dr. Naylor James Naylor and I had a 12d sent from Yorke from Henry Gyles to be drunke amongst us and this night we were togeather to spend the 12d. Afterwards I went into Thomas Harrisons and Thomas wife was not well and if I would sepnd 2d he would spend 3d so we sent for drinke and I was very ernest to have John Pottr there and went and fetched hime so he and John Hasleden and I we spent each 2d a piece.

-31st. St. Andrews day.

I went to Bein forlonge to Ann Greiswort to cast up her accounts she made much of me and I came home.

It will be frequently noted that strict Puritan as Lowe was he frequently attaches the names of saints' days to the entries of his diary.

December 1664.

-3. Saturday.

My Mr sent little Thomas to me with commodities and I thought he had overcharged them and it trouble me very much.

-8. thursday.

William Key came to me to have me go with him to Wiggan to cast up some accounts between him and Mr. Totty about the buying and selling of beasts as I promised to go in the evening because I could not deferr my Mr service but I should do it at night so this afternoone I went to Bein forlonge and cald of hime and we went togathr and ware most part of night and in the othr morninge came away but there was some differences between them and we did nothinge to purpose.

49

-9.

When I came home friday Mrs. ffinch sent for me to Raph Hasleden and intrested me to bringe her home att night which I promised to doe.

-18. lords day.

I went to the funerall of Henry Ashton son of William de Whitleighe greene att comeing home there was Tho Harrison John Pottr and some others and we cald att Heapyes and spent 2d apiece so came hme and at John Jenkins we did as so before we parted and so bid farewell to one another when twopeny flaggon was concluded.

-19. Munday.

Robert Nelson came into shop and through my importunocie was prveild with to let me understand the words used in stanching bloud which privatly usd amongst country persons not pubickly knowen and the words are to be seriously said 3 times together and so hath beene used to staunch bloud said 3 times together.

There was a babe in bethlem borne.
And christiand in the water of flem Jordan.
The watr it was both wild and wood.
The child it was both meeke and good
Stauch bloud in gods name.

Say three times togeather.

In the 'Gentleman' Magazine for July, 1835, will be found a somewhat similar charm for stauchblood taken from an old book of medical recipes written in 1610. This runs as follows;-

To staunch bloude.
There were three Maryes over the floude;
The one did stand, the other ftente bloude:
Then bespoke Mary that Jesus Christ bore,
Defende gods forbod thou shoudeste bleede **anye** more.

The three Marys here named were probally the Virgin Mary, the Egyptian Mary, and Mary Magdelene. Whether these words are to be spoken as an exorcism or worn as a charm is mentioned. Similar 'charmes' are quoted in Harland and Wilkinson" Folk Lore, page 77.

-21. Wedensday.

I was with John Pottr and Tho Harrison att Tankerfeilds with the Harthman that came to view Harthes in Ashton and spent 4d.

-24.

I was this night with Matthew Raphes and John Hasleden in Joshua Naylors on purpose to take house for Joshua and we did take a house of Mathew Raphes. On this night I saw a comett in the aire a starr with a traine along with it.

This comet will be found referred to in Martindale's Diary (page 179): 'There was a dreadful comet (somethought two or more: See Wing's Computatio Catholica) in November and December 1664Ó. John Evelyn, in his diary, notes the appearence of a comet in the year 1680:- 'This evening looking out of my chaber window towards the west, I saw a meteor of an obsecure bright colour, very much in shape like the blade of a sword, the rest of the skie very serene and cleare. What this may portend God onely knows: but such another phenomenon I remember to have seen in 1640, aboute the Triall of the Great Earle of Strafford, preceeding our bloudy Rebellion. I pray avert his judgements. We had had severall comets, of late which tho' I believe appeare from natural causes and of themselves operate not yet I cannot despise them. They may be warnings from God, as they commonly are forerunners of his animadversions. After many daies and many nights of snow, cloudy and dark weather, the comet was very much wasted.'

-28. Wedensday.

I was envited to supr to Rogr Naylors and went.

-29. Thursday.

Att night I went with William Hasleden to be all night att Thomas Heyes and in the other morneing I came home.

Jennery 1664-5.

-1.

I went to Leigh and schoole Mr had gotton me leave to goe with hime to Mr. Woods to be all night but I refused to goe for this time. Att noone my sistr Ellin came to me in the church yard and we both of us went to see my fathr and mothers grave and stayd a while and both wept. Went to my sistrs Katherins and we had 2d in ale and so parted. I went into church and there was given some christenings and I went out againe for my Mr son was to come with me and dayes ware short so I resolved to come home.

-2. Munday.

I went to the funerall of Jane Pottr John Pottr daughter of Lilly lane who was this day interred at winwicke and att or comeing home I was with John Pottr of Ashton and James Low and some others and we went togather into a house cald

Spoilers in Newton spent 4d and so went home. When I came home Thomas Tickle was come out of Renford with John Haselden and was at John Jenkins drinkeinge they sent for me and I went but it cost me nothinge for Ralph and John spent either of them 12d.

-6. friday.

I went to Bein forlonge and John Jenkins wife went with me.

-8. lords day.

Att noone I went home with Robert Rosbothome to dinner and this night Thomas Smith and I went to gather to John Taylors in Goleborne and heard Mr Woods preach and we had sacrement. We came home this night.

-9. Munday.

I was sent to the funerall of my brothers child cald Ralph [he] dyd att Thos Gerards house in Windle and was buryd att St Ellins this same day.
-10 tusday.

Thos Tickle came to me out of Reinford to go with him to old Mr Woods who was att John Robinsons he would receive sacrement I went with hime but all was done before we came and we stayd all night there.

-14. saturday.

Thomas Smith and I went to younge Mr. Woods in Atherton where he lived with his wife in Gyles Greenes house. As we went we cald of John Hampson in Hindley who brought us to Mr. Woods house and sent where Mr Woods was and John and I stayd awhile then parted.

The residence of Rev James Wood, the minister of the old Chowbent Chapel is exactly given in this interesting entry by Roger Lowe.

-15th.

We all went to Houghton Chappell and heard Mr. Lever preach. Att noone John Hampson tooke me home with hime to dinner the next day we intended home but Mr. Woods would not suffer us but all afternoone we shufled att table in bent there was Tho Moxon and I and Petr Twisse playd with Mr. Woods and his partners we beat them. The other day we came home Ann Woods and Mr. Woods maid came with us and att Ashton we tooke them into Alehouse and promisd them to come to them att Widow Clarkes in Windle but I could not.

-29. lords day.

Henry Gerard sent for me to procure him a man to go to Lancr and thence to London which I did I get John Jenkinson and this afternoone I went with hume to Bein forlonge but Henry Gerard was not att home and it was supposed he had gotton one.

52

ffebruery 1664-5.

-8. Wedensday.

      John Naylor wife of Edg greene sent for me thither they had buryd a lad cald Joseph Day before.

-9. Thursday.

      I went to Blacky Hurst to the funerall of Thomas Blakeburne who was buryd at Winwicke.

-10. friday.

      Emm Pottr and I fell out and

-11. Saturday.

      Being in a sad fitt I composed these verses followeing in thought of somethinge her sister would speake against me on Shrove tusday night att John Jenkinsons upon wh Emm and I parted

Well I'me content tho fortune on me frowne
God will me raise tho the world would cast me downe
And I with patience will their malace bear
who seek to defame me nay do curse and swear
& lye in oposition what theyve said
but vengence will at last light on their head
let world say best and worst all is one to me
in time my quarrell will revenged be
till then Ill waite and onely seeke to God
yt heele be pleased to remove this flicting rod
and I doe hope yt I shall live to see
myself inlarged and freed from callumme
and they are yt are ye actors of mr greefe
and they cry out and yet find no reliefe
But this I wish not: o that they migt be
preseved from all such kind of miserie.

This day my old fathr Storrope came to town and moved me to goe along with hime to Gawthers I did he spent his 6d on me.

-15. Wedensday.

      I went to Bein forlonge to Greinsworth to set down accounts for her.

-19. lords day.

      I went to Winwicke to see John Hasledens love.

-26. lords day.

I went to Winwicke there was no preachinge att Ashton.

-27. Munday.

Mr. Robt Greinsworth came from London and cald on me and forced me to go with him to Bein forlonge so I gat him to gat John Jenkins to come with me because it was night and I would come so John and I stayd till 12 o'clock in night drinking and afterwards we came home and ....

-28. tusday.

I was sick all day but ere night the lord restored me.

March 1664-5.

-2. thursday.

Henry Houghton came to me to have me make a lease for hime of his house between Mr. Byrom de Byrom and hime.

-3. friday.

I went to his house to buy a heifer in calve and I bought her for 39s. and he was to keepe her a month.

-14th. tusday.

Henry Houghton came to me and William Crouchley and had me to go with them to Parr hall to seale lease to Mr. Byrom. He saeled it and Mr. Edwd Byrom and his two Brothrs yt ware distracted went and brought us to an Ale house where we stayd drinkeinge a good while then we passed for home and att Ashton I mett with some Leigh people yt ingaged me to be with them and I was with them.

-24th. friday.

My Mr came to towne and he had told me yt he had heard many things of me and wished for me for my good to be cautious he spoke very loveingly to me and I was afraid before he came lest he would have beene angry.

-26. lords day.

I went to Leigh and John Chadocke and I walked after Broakeside in Slatefields att noone discousing about my effaires and my Mr att our returne into Towne I went into George Morris house to old Mr. Woods who was there and stayd awhile then went into Church and Mr. Crampton preached and I was glad of it.

The Rev. Thomas Crompton was minister of Astley Chapel from 1631 to 1691. He is described as 'a very honest minister (only he kept not the last fast).'

-28. tusday.

I was envited and went to John Hasledens marriage att Winwicke was his man.

Aprill 1665.

-2. lords day

John Hasleden and I went to the Lees beyond Holland to heare Mr. Baldwin preach and att Hugh Wortington in Holland we ware to meet Thomas Tickle and other Reinford men which we did and stayd drinkinge of 8d and so went to one Mr. Lawrence Hallewell where Mr. Baldwin was and preacht in the forenoon but we ware prevented with some women that came into house and some of them ware papists so we ware forced to come home before latr sermon was preached and att Holland we stayd drinkeinge of 12d and then parted home but Thomas Tickle paid it.
Richard Baldwin was returned in the Church Survey of 1649 as minister of Holland, near Wigan, which had been made into a separate parish by order of Parliament. He was described as 'a very able minister of honest life.'

-3. Munday.

Mr. Banistr de Banke came through Ashton being slain att fforest of dellimore being accompanied with store of gentry. Att sun sett this eveninge Ann Johnson departed this life.

Mr. J.P. Earwaker writes of this entry in the diary:- In the orbituary, under the same date, there is more information given, to the effect that 'Mr. Henry Banister was drawn on a litter dead through the town being slain by Colket att Sir Philip Edgerton att a race on Forest of Delamere.' These entries are exceedingly interesting as they confirm the account of the death of Henry Banaster as given in the Banaster pedigree and correct in the detail where it is stated that he was slain in the Isle of Man. Henry Banaster of Bank Esq. who is here referred to was the son of Henry Banaster of bank Esq. (who died 1641) he married Dorothy daughter of Roger Nowell of Read, Esq. She survived her husband and was living in 1676. he was buried April 11, 1665 leaving no issue. His murderer Colket or Colcoth was condemned and executed at Chester for the murder.

-5. Wedensday.

I went to Standish to the funerall of Ann Johnson and I came into the church when Mr. Bowker was preachinge for it was day of humiliation for the kings nevy set out att aftr she was interred and was come into house where we dranke and saw how they intended to serve us who ware come out of Ashton with every one a loaf John Pottr and I ware somewhat hungery and angry we took flight to Wiggan to Eles Leighes house and there refreshed ourselves.

The 'Kings Navy' was then engaged in war with the Dutch. The occasion is noticed by Peyps and Evelyn, the latter stating in his diary that it was the day of humiliation 'for successe of this terrible was begun doubtless at secret instigation of the French to weaken the States and Protestant interest. Prodigious preparations on both sides.'

-11. tusday

        I went to the funerall of Grace Gerard to Winwicke who was there interred.

-16. Saturday.

        I went with John Hasleden and his wife to Reinford to Henry Sephton and

-18. Munday

        We came home togethr.

-23. lords day.

        I went to Leigh.

-28. friday.

        I was in greefes all day in concideration of my charge for fear shop should not answr my Mr expectation beig now to be cast up but my trust is in the lord who nevr failes those who trust in hime.

-29. Saturday.

        Petr Leyland came to towne and wished me to goe bringe him towards home and in William Knowes fieiled cald horse head undr banke we sat downe and he told me his troubles in regard of his daughtrs distempr wo was falling sicknes and his two sonnes that the one was void of a callinge and the other weake and infirme and amidst or talke we both fell fast asleepe.

-30. lords day.

        Mr. Pilkington person of Gresson prescht here and att night I went down to hime he was att Thomas Naylors and envited hime to take a flaggon. We went to Thomas Leeches and stayd awhile and so parted.

    Mr. James Pilkington was rector of Croston at the time of the diarist.

May 1665.

-1. Monday.

        This morninge I went with Thomas Harrison with a sterle to Lodge to have her scord.

-2. Tusday.

My Brother with his wife came with his beasts removing out of Windle into Houghton to Dazy Hillocke to Petr Rylands house he yt was the sequestor and I brought them towards Houghton and I was exceedingly troubled in my mind for my poor Brother.

-7. lords day.

Mr. Byrom came to towne Mr. Bowkr preachd and att night John Jenkinson and I went with Mr Byrom to bringe hime towards home.

-11th. May.

My Mr. came to Ashton and told me I must come home and bid me to set all things in ordr this was sad newes but its good to submitt to god in his verious providences.

-15. Munday night.

I went be all night att John Robbinson's there was old Mr. Woods and Mr. Martindale.

-16. tusday.

I went to Bein forlonge and this night I was in sad condition by reason of Ann Taylors comeing to Ellin Harison and telling her stories of mein so much as Emm Pottr beinge att Halsall I was almost intendinge to have gone in night I was sadly troubled and was att this time very vehement in effection towards her.

-17. Wedensday.

I went about twelve a clocke att noone to meet her and upon the Brow this side Orrell more short of the barne that stands by itselfe in the valley there is a ditch I sate where I might see all the moor ovr desireing to see my wished sight it rained and after I was almost tyred in waiteing I resolved to go down brow towards Barne and in goeinge I mett with Devid Pendlebury an Ashton man homewards so I asked him whether he would go spend this 1d att Skenneing Johns who said he would. We ware no sooner gotten into house and had a flaggon but Mr. Leigh schoolmaster of Ashton came in and it was a rainy day and my expectations was frustrate that troubled me much so we stayd 2 or 3 flaggons and then parted and I came home and she was come before me and was undrest but notwithstanding taylor had done her indeavor to incense her against me yet in vaine and I was glad to see her.

-28. lords day.

I went to Leigh and had a little Hare for children att noone I went to John Chaddockes and he and I went a walking and discourseing about me what I

57

should doe in answr to myselfe betweene me and My Mr. att night my dame would have me take mare home with me and litle Thomas behind me and so we did litle Thomas was troubled with sores and they would have me goe with him to Marklands the other morneing which we did and lest ware we rid off att widow Clarkes till we returned back from Marklands so att or return to Ashton I went to see how he could ride and brought him to further ende of towne greene and so left hime.

June 1665.

-i. Thursday.

     I went to Sarah Jenkinsons brotherley and brothr to Henry ffrances in Pemberton to see the burneing well and we had 2 eggs which was so done by no materiall fire we returnd backe to Watts in Whitleige greene and there I had information that Robert Pendleberry had sent for ribbininge to marle pitt which causd my hast to shop and thence to Roberts.

     The Burning Well near Pemberton no longer exists. It was caused by a temporary escape of carburetted hydrogen gas. It is described in Baines (vol. ii, 189, new ed.), who quotes the following from an old geography;- 'At Antcliffe two miles from Wigan, is a very raere phenomenon much visited by curious travellers, which is called the Burning Well. 'Tis cold and hath no smell, yet so strong a vapour of sulphour issues out with its water that upon putting a lighted candle to it it instantly catches the flame like spirits, which last several hours, and sometimes a day in calm weather, with a heat fierce enough to make pot boil, though the water itself remains cold, and will not burn when taken out of the well any more than the mud of it.' A similar well existed in Derby-lane about a mile from Hindley Hall which has long since been buried beneath cartloads of rubbish. - (Leyland's Memorials of Hindley.)'

-3 Saturday night.

     James Jenkins and I went all up and downe to find John Jenkins who was suposd to be drowned but att 12 clocae in night we found him fast asleep amidst town feild.

-5. Munday.

     Daniell Chadocke was come to towne to meete Mr. Taylor who was come over and gone to his unkle Stirrope we went Daniell Chadocke John Jenkinson and I to Goleborne Copp and sent to Mr. Taylor to have hime come thithr and when he came we went to the Alley and played att bowles and annon Mr. Pottr came and Mr Widowes John Jenkins and I beat Mr Pottr Mr Taylor and Mr. Chaddocke in each of them 4d in ale.

-6. tudsady.

I went to Warrington to pay some money and Mr. Worrall was very respectful to me and comforted me very much for days to come and so did Mr Scofeild.

-7. Wedensday.

I was sent for to Bein forlonge to Ann Greinsworth and went.

-11. lords day.

In the afternoone I went to Neawton to hear Mr. Tayler preach I was very pensive and sad att this time in consideration of my condition in this world but God is the rocke to which I hold and the watrs of consolation is still distilled from hime against the greatest discourgaements.

-13. tusday. I was sent for to Bein forlonge and I went.

-18. lords day.

I went to Wiggan and heard Mr. Kenion pastor of Prestwidge most excelantly preach.

-19.

I went to Leigh and was ill wett.

-22. thursday.

I went to Leigh and had broowed six pound for my Mr. against Chester faire.

-24. Saturday.

In the afternoone Mr. Leandrs came and wild me goe to Goleborne Copp to bowle and I see a game or two of bowld and came home againe.

-25. lords day.

Mr. Taylor preachd att Ashton I went to Bein forlonge this night to make streight Annes accounts for she was efraid her brother would come from London.

-27. tusday.

I went to John Robbinsons for his daughter widow Jaxon had envited me upon a privat account to ecqueint me of some private business and this afternoone I had spent with Mr. Barker vicker of Standish and Mr. Leandrs after I had parted with them I went towards John Robinsons and was all night and the mattr she had to equaint me was that if I ware ....
Mr Martindale had and could provide a good wife for me a woman in Chestr his one sister hey Major Jollyes daughter hath £120 to her portion I was glad of the business and had some hopes of freedom of my Mr.

The writer in the note if the 'Manchester Courier' says that both these passages (15th. May and the above date) refer to that period of Adam Martindale's life when he was finding 'good employment bith ministeriall and mathematicall.' The first reference is explained by a passage in Martindale's Diary page 177, from which it appears that after Christmas, 1664, he was received as tutor to the family of Sir Richard Hoghton, of Hoghton Tower. Martindale's prescence in Roger Lowe's neighbourhood is due to its being the home of his sister Margaret, who, in the year 1665 'died in Ashton-in-Makerfield and was there buryd' (page 179. The second reference made by Lowe to Martindale find confirmation at page 234 of the Diary of the latter where the writer speaks of lodging at 'my brother [Nathan] Jollie's house in Chester.' Jollie was brother in half blood to Mrs. Martindale.

-28. Wedensday.
          Bedtime in the morninge I came hime amd Mr Bowkr sent for me and we ware togathr a certaine time.

-29th. thursday.
          I was with the white smiths of Ashton and made an agreement for them to goe to counsell with about their trade. This night I went to Robert Rosbothams and was there all night and Richard Orme asked me to make a pair of Indentured and two bonds and he gave me directions about them. I was at this time sadly troubled concering Mrs. Rosthornes death who died at Bold Hall where she was borne and ther carried to Lodge in Chowbent and upon the 31 of June was interred att Leigh she was carried dead from Bold to Atherton in a horse litter

John Atherton of Atherton Esquire married Mary daughter of Richard Bold of Bold, Esquire (by Ann his wife daughter of Peter Legh of Lyme Knight). According to Dugdales Vistitation entry in the diary his widow appears to have married ..... Rawsthorne, esquire. The 'Mr. Atherton of Atherton and Bewsey' whom the diarist calls the son of Mrs. Rawsthorne was Richard Atherton Esqu.ire who, succeeded to Atherton on the death of his father and inherited Bewsey from Dame Margaret Ireland who died 1675. He was born 22 September 1656, and on 27th Novmber 1676 married at Warrington Isabell daughter of Robert Holt of Castleton and Stubley by whom he had John Atherton his successor and other issue. He married secondly Agnes daughter of Miles Dodding of Cornishead Esqr. by whom he had no issue. In 1671 Mr. Atherton was elected M.P. for Liverpool but was unseated on petition; he was Mayor of that town in 1684. On 22nd. John 1684, he was knighted at Winsor by the King. Sir Richard's grandson Richard Atherton of Atherton and Bewsey Esq dying on the 14th. November, 1726 left an only child Elizabeth who was married to Robert Gwillym of Walford co. Hereford Esq, in whose family the estates remained until the marriage in 1764 of Henrietta Maria Gwillam (heiress to her brother Atherton Leigh Gwilliam who died s.p.) to the Hon.

Thomas Powys afterwards Lord Lilford, father by her son of Lord Lilford and of the present Bishop of Sodor and Man. - Manchester Courier Notes.

July 1665.

-i. lords day.

Mr. Hanmer preached att Ashton and att night Thos Smith and I went to John Robbinsons and there repeated both sermons.

-6. friday.

Anne Barrow sent for me she livd with her sister Margret Naylor on Edg greene and there I repeated Mr. Hamners sermons.

-11. wedensday.

I went to Leigh.

-30. lords day.

I went to Wiggan Joshua Naylor and John Hasleden went along with me and when we came to Eles Leighes we stayd and had each a cuppe of ale and then I left him drinkeinge and I went into church and att nonne when I came out they were gone homewards I was all this time in expectation of my Mr. to come cast up shop and he came not which troubled me very much.

August 1665.

-6. Lords day.

Edward Hayhurst junior of Chowbent sent for me this morneinge and wishd me to goe with hime to Denton green he wood Tho Hollands daughter and I promised hime I would he hyrd me a horse and we went to Denton greene to one Darbishires ale house and sent for her but she was gone to church and the wife sent for us so we went and stayd there till she came home and ware much made of but we had a rainy eveninge home.

-8. tusday.

Richard Orme came and I went with him and John Pottr to Windle to seale Indentures I had made for to bynd Henry Orme prntice to Josiah Clarke sadlr when he was bound we rid upp to Denton greene for John Pottr I thanke hime let me rid behind hime and att Denton greene we stayd and playd three games of bowles and spent each 2d and so we partd and ware ill wett.

-12.

I went with Mr. Launders to Gleborne Copp and playd att bowles.

-13. lords day.

Edmund Hayhurst came and enjoined me to go to Mr Sorowcold to move him to act the business for him for a mariage.

-14.

Betime the morneinge I went to Mr. Serowcold upon that business att my comeing home I went to Winwick to the funerall of a child of Josiah Naylor and John Pottr and I went with Thomas Lyon to Hoornes greene where ere we pted there was some difference between Thomas Lyon and Darbishire who ware ingaged in a game of Bowles and could not agree and in parlor where we ware was Mr. Mather an attorney that defended Thomas Lyons case and provoked us to much passion but John Pottr and I ware for peace and this Mathr puts us all in one and intends to sue us.

-23 day.

I went to Warrington and John Pottr too on purpose to know his pleasure and att home att Thomas Kerfootes I cald he and his wife had spoke much for me so I gat them to go along with me which they did and Mather said he would be civill with me; that was all I went to seeke John Pottr and found him not until I was prting with towne where I found him in Mathrs sistrs house so went to his hot house and spent 2d and he let me ride behind him home we ware both exceedingly hungry and cald in Heapy's in Neawton and whiles we are eating and drinkinge we had almost fallen out about presbittery and Episcopecie.

-20. lords day.

I was with young Mr. Woods att old John Robinsons and I was all night with Mr. Woods preached and he would not let me pass home and the othr day he came to towne with me.

-27. lords day.

I went to Wigin Thomas Smith with me and we cald of Robert Rosbothom and he and his wife went along with us I told Thomas Smith my greevences about Emm and me falling out and her sister so we cast that Thomas should come on thursday after to Tankerfields and send for Emm and there conclude peace att night Robert and wife ware gone home and Thomas and I followed and we called at Adamsons att Goose greene and spent 3d so we parted to Roberts where they ware att supr we stayd and so came home.

-30. Wedensday.

I received a lettr from Thomas Johnson of Laverpoole and a lad with a horse where he desired me to go with the lad and pay James Boydells for Caridge of wine [or wire] and receive it from Thomas which I did and when I was upon Louton Comon I tooke horse and went to Leigh and gat some goods and so passed away back againe.

September 1665.

-3. lords day.

I went to Billinge Chappell in the afternoone with John Potter and others and we went and called on Henry Birchall in the fields and spent each 2d and so went to chappell. When eveninge service was done Mr. Blackburne envited me into house but I could not goe but desired excuse. We came back againe to Henry Birchall and stayd awhile and so came for home.

-12. Tusday.

In the afternoone I went to John Robbinson there sent was a private day and a sacremet Old Mr. Woods preached I came as he was preaching and I received the sacrement the lord sanctifie it unto me. There was Mary Barkr there to whom I had some thoughts to intended to sent Tho Smith to speak my business. This night Thomas Smith was made up to Eles Lealand on old John Robbinsons chambr.

-23. Wedensday.

My Mr. had sent me a very shrewd message to Peter Higson and I framd a letter and got Thomas Smith to go speake my busines he went on St. Mathews day and My Mr. was very sore displeased.

This is another instance of the occasions reference to saints days, although the diarist was a staunch Puritan.

-29.

I went with Edward Hayhurst to Denton greene he hired a horse.

October 1665.

-8. lords day night.

Thomas Smith asked me to goe with hime to Peter Lealands which I did Sarah Hasleden asked me to come to their house which I did and there was Rosted goose and I eate my supr.

-9. Munday.

I went with Thomas Smith to Winwick to his marieage with Eles Lealand att night I was envited to old Peter p goe hoem with them which I did and stayd supr.

-13. friday night.

I went with old William Hasleden and his two horses with two strangers to Liverpoole within night mcerely out of my one mind.

63

-23. munday.

I went into Hayddock to seaverall houses to gett moneys but I got none.

-30th tusday.

I went with John Pottr Richard Asmull John Darbishire to Winwick to meet Mr. Mather and that threatened to sue us and for which I was under great trouble but home we came thither he was att Neawton att Rothwells so we all went thithr and sent for hime but his demands was so extraordinarie that we all came home very sad.

November 1665.

-i Wedensday.

I went to Leigh and when I came into towne I found Raph Jenkins in the stocks and a fire upon Crosse by hime he had been all night. Att my comeing home I gate a horse and resolved to goe to Winstanley to speake and move Mr. Blakeburne to be my freind about Mathers busines. We came down to Humphrey Athertons sate in the parlor by the fire and talked a great while of everything somethinge and he showd me very great respect to me and he would doe what lye in him to doe for me.

Roger Lowe refers to an old insitution in the town of Leigh, now happily forgotton by even the proverbial oldest inhabitants. Confinement in the stocks was a punishment which the local justices could award for almost every offence and a night spent in the open air with feet fast was no means penance for a drunken debauch or the indefinite crime of being a rogue and a vagabond. The stocks in which Ralph Jenkins was seen by the diarist appears to have been in the Market-place. The 'cross' was the market cross which probally occupied the position of the present obilisk, although no evidence but the above entry can be given to prove that Leigh Market-place possessed the common ornament of most county towns. This evidence, is, too very weak. On the site occupied by the old police courts in King Street up to little more that 50 years ago, stood the stocks and dungeons but there is no evidence that the stocks when they were removed occupied the same position that they did when the diarist was serving his apprenticeship to the Leigh mercer.

-5. lords day.

I went to Billinge chapel and heard Mr. John Blackburne preach he shewd me a lettr he had receivd from Mathr and he promisd on reverse the busines that terme and Mr. John told me he would not be wantinge in any thinge for me I dined at John Cowlys.

-7. tusday night.

I went to Thomas Smiths he lived att Cookes house near to Robert Rosbothoms house I was there att night with hime. The other morneinge Thomas and I went to his fatherleys Peter Lealand to get hime to goe to Watts house to see if he could take it for them.

> The expression 'fatherleys' is used for father-in-law, Thomas Smith having married Alice Leyland in the previous month. In another entry the word 'brotherleys' occurs as brother-in-law.

-14. tusday.

My Mr came and I was in a sad sorowfull estate for fear of being undrhand my Mr proffed to let me have goods and to free me.

-17. firday.

I rid before Sarah Hasleden to Leigh to see my accounts I was charged with 205li. and I profited 48li. I was glad then I went with Sarah to Hugh Hindleys for his daughtr was lyeing in. Att our returne againe my Mr was proffering shop to me and I expected of it tho I was very sorowful yet my trust is in God.

> Roger records this day his unexpected freedom from his apprenticeship. The diarist is now an Ashton tradesman in business on his own account, bound only to his old master for the goods he owed.

-20th, Munday.

I went to Warrington and bought ... and othr comodities.

-24.

My Mr came and cast up shop and thought I had beene far behind hand but on the 17 day I had Sarah Hasleden went to Leigh and I went to perfect all accounts and I had gained my Mr 48li in a year and a halfe and I was very gald. I went with Sarah to Hugh Hindleys for his daughter was lying in but when I came to Leigh againe my Mr proffrd me to trust me for the goods in Ashton and to give me my time which I expected of God hath beene with me hitherto his name be glorified.

December 1665.

-20.

I went to Leigh and gat my Mr to let me have some comodities I wanted which he did and sent his sone to bringe them for me I was att this time sadly troubled for feare of miscarying and knew not how to get cloth and things yet god raisd up freinds for me a Yorkeshireman came through towne and proffrd to let me have cloth for three months.

-21.

I went to Warrington and Thomas Peake was very earnest with me to have me journey man for him in Laverpoole which I denyd I bought some comodities upon trust of Mr. Worrell so came home.

-26. tusday.

I went with John Pottr and Thomas Harison to Manchester. We ware up very early and gat to Boothestowne by day came [to] Earldomes and spent each 2d a piece for I begun to be very feeble and then we came to Manchester and in the first place we went to church and I lookd about us and at anon the quiristrs came and we stayd morninge prayer I was exceedinglie taken with the mellodie. Then we three haveing each seaverall busines done first I showd Thomas Harrison Mr. Sandiforths where he was to doe his business and he had and I went and enquired of hme as soone as he see me very kindlie tooke me in and would not let passe till I had dined with hime and so did Thomas too but this while we had lost John Pottr and made much labour to find hime and whiles we ware finding hime I gat business pfected with Mr. Howham but when we found John Pottr he was very angry att us then we went altogether to ahouse John Jenkins brought us to where we ware troubled with fowle sheets all night but all this day we could not perfect nothing of John Pottrs business which was to be done with one Robert Johnson a draper who was out of town but in far of night we went to his house when he heard of his comeinge home by John Hopwood to whom we ware ingaged much to gat his business done.

> The diarist on several occasions records his curiosity to hear 'organes' and music (Winwick 17th. March, 1662-3; Manchester, 22nd. December, 1665, the above date; and at Chester, 28th. June 1666). These entries may illustrate the rigor with which music had been shut out during the Commonwealth. The church visited in Manchester was St. Peter's Collegiate Church now the cathedral of the diocese.

-27.

We sat out of Manchester and John Pottr was not well and besides he over went Thomas and me to Earloms and never gave us word all which troubled me exceedinglie in my mind but we came to Earloms and there we ware merry and thence we came to Leigh and at widow Ranikers we stayd and spent each of us 2d a piece from thence we came home but by the way he had a little onhappy discourses with religion as too of we have been overtaken with too much passion for each of us ware of different judgements and each would vindicate his own way and many times fall into exceedinge passion tho it never occasiond is to love the less which I often marked as a providence of god for I received so many singular favours from them as caused me to love them entirely. Att our coeming into Tho Harrisons we found an old man and his wife that Thomas was ingaged too we went to Alehouse and ware very merry togather.

66

-30. Saturday.

Robt Rosbotham sent for me Mr. Woods was come to his house and I went and Mr. Woods preachd. I lay att Thomas Smiths who lived then at Cookes house.

Jenuery 1665.

-i. Munday.

I went to Nicholas Croft to bid him fatch the cow.

-2. tusday.

I went huntinge and the hare tooke into rabits holes and I was exceedingly wearied.

-3. Wedensday.

I went to Leigh to speake to Mr. Swift who was come and gone againe. I was sadlie troubled I came away by my sister Ellin and stayd awhile and so came to Richard Ormes for I should have stayd there all night Richard was not att home and so I came home.

-4. thursday.

I gat Thomas Harrison to goe along with me to peter Lealands Haddocke woods to looke att chest for me I wish to buy.

-10. wedensday.

I went hinteinge awhile and then came home.

-15. Munday.

I hired Tho Leach horse and rid to Standish on purpose to buy a suite of brown shagge but there was none I came back to Wiggan and stayd to speake with Mr. Pilkinton about mony that a servent of his owed my Mr. I had the compeine of one Hugh Toppin of Warrington who told me there was the head of some Christian lay bare to publike view above ground and that it waa charitie to bury it which I said I would doe.

-16. tusday.

I went to bury it. It lay in the high lane as one gets to barly mans just att the crosse cawsaw it in my hands to the dungeons slift of the towne field and there buryd it digd the hole with my fingers. It was supposed to have beene a Scot and there slaine when duke Hamilton invaded England.

Cawsaw is probally causeway. This entry is strangely enough the only direct or indirect reference to the Civil Wars, which occurs in Roger Lowe's diary.

-17. Wednesday.

I went to Warrington and payd Richard Worrell all that I owed hime I bought me a new hatt and stockins. Came to Neawton and there spent 4d.

-19. friday.

I went to the funerall of old Mrs. Birch being envited by John Jenkins.

-23.

John Jenkinson desired me to goe with his child to Winwick to stand as a godfather Mr. Bowkr had faild and could not come so he intrested me to go with hime which I did and we went into Clarke's att after the christening and spent 3s. Then we went to widow Barkrs and we spent othr 3s. but it was very rugged night and darke yet John and I came home.

ffebruerie 1665.

-2. ffriday.

I went with John Potter and his wife to his wives sisters who lived att a place called Lawnes and we ware much made of att after diner we went up to Holland to Thomas Prescotts and ware merry and then Humphry Naylors and stayd awhile and so came to Lawnes againe where we all of us supt and then John Potter and I came home and Honest Thomas Birchall and would not leave us but came home with us but James Low stayed all night there and left us which was not well taken. Att this time there was one Gaskell who owned Tower hill house above the Lawnes had hanged himselfe.

-3. Saturday.

Emm and I ware exceedingly falne out which greeved me sore and she was gone with Ann Taylor towards Golebourne. Coppe and I got Mathew Turton to go with me and we went and took them in Cepp house I sat down with them but shee would not be moved I spent 12d and was more greeved than before.

-4. lords day.

I went with John Potter to Billinge chappell and att noone we came to Henry Birchalls to diner where we stayd all afternoone and drunke.

-5. Munday.

I was sent for to my sister Ellin who was brought to bed and was likely for death and when I came to her she was speechles which greeved me sore I stayd all the afternoone and att night after sun goe downe I parted and came home about 8 of clock in night when I was gone she dyd.

68

-6. tusday.

I went to the funerall of my deare sister and her child was christened the same day she was buryd at Winwicke p Mr. Potter. Mr. Watt came to funerall to accompanie me which I was ingaged for. My sisters child was named Rogr.

-10. Saturday.

Mr. Bowker came to Ashton and I went to bring hime to Nicholas Burscoes house for there he was all night and in the was we fell out extremelie about religion but one [on].

11th. lords day.

In the morninge when he came to Ashton back againe he sent for me and we ware friends.

-18. lords day.

I went to Winwicke with John Potter. We came home at noone Mr. Potter would have me to dinner.

-19. Munday.

I was sadly troubled in my thoughts by reason of the debts I did owe and for fear lest I should miscarry. Now the Lord help me and be my helper till death and att death now the lord bring me out of these troubles in his good time.

March 1665.

-6. tusady.

Att night I went to Robert Rosbothoms and was there all night.

-7. Wedensday.

I went to John Robbinsons and was there all night.

-8. thursday.

I went to John Blakburn to Winstanley to treate with hime about Mathrs busines who had sent to him so he sent to me to have me come to him and concerninge this busines I was much ingaged to honest Mr. Blakeburne I envited Mr. Blakeburne downe to Humphrey Winstanleys we went I told him they had assessed me in Ashton for a psonell estate and I had none so he told me what course to take which I did. After we had drunke awhile I parted. Att my comeinge to Ashton I resolved to set forward to Leigh and from thence to Light Okes but when I came to Leigh Sr Henry Slater was in towne I gat my Mr. to go with me to hime and so ecqueinted hime with my busines. He moved me to come the day ensuing and it should be done I parted and went from Leigh to Mr. James Woods house who livd then at James Dawsons in Atherton and was in weake condition. We ware a little mery the othr day I stayd till noone redinge a booke of martirs and then departed to my brothers who livd aat Rylands house at Dazy Hillock and stayd there awhile there and so went to Leigh where I found Sr Henry Slater and Mr. Rosthorne att Robbinsons and Thomas Naylor who was Sr Henrys clarke made great profesions of love to me writt me an order and caused it to be signed by two justices and would have nothing for this labour so I came home. I found the lord a helper of me in my distress His Holy name be praised.

-12. Munday.

I was advised to give this order I had gotten from the Justices to the Constable which I did and went with the Constable to Thomas Naylors because he had causd me to be layd.

-14 Wedensday.

I went to Warrington to pay some monys I owd to Schofield.

-18 lords day.

Emm and I fell out this eveninge I went to old John Robinsons was all night Old Mr. Woods was there and preached and there was Mary Barton there all night and I intended to send to herr which I did. Edmund Winstanley wife the othr day.

There are several iteresting local references in the above entry. 'Light Oaks' still remains at the extreme end of Bedford and is a well known farm house though now very considerably altered and modernized.

25 March 1666.

- I went being lorrds day to the funerall of old Allins wife who was interred at Winwick. I was with John Potter and Thomas Harrison with some others we spent 3d apeece att after the funerall and thence came to Rothwells in Neawton and spent each othr 3d besides and so we parted hime I was ill all night but the lord had mercie on me the othr morninge.

-27. tusday.

I went to Laverpoole to but comodities I light of Mr. Renyolds Sr Williams steward who enjoined me to come to Mr. Christians to hime. We spent most of the afternoone in drinkinge I parted and came to Mr. Johnsons shop where I gate some busines done and in the doeinge of my affairs I mett with Mr. Swift whome I intended to go too. He livd in Chester he was a Bristoll merchant and traded in Bristoll goods I was to goe to him the next morneinge which I did and went up to his chabr where he lyed and causd a pottle of butt end ale to come up so I gat my busines done and then set forward for Ashton and made Highton my way. Cald of Mr. Low the vicar and we went to the Clarkes house and ware merry a while and then I came home.

-30. friday night.

I was all night att Robert Rosbothoms. This night Raph Low son of dam and hanged himself in shippon before beasts.

April 1666.

-13th good friday.

John Hasleden wife was undr the pangs of childbirth and they sent for me to pray by her which I did att this time I was in a great sadnes not knoweing what to doe.

-16. Munday

I went to Leigh to pay some monys to my Mr. and he was out towne William Dewnell was in town about his daughters marriage with Mr. Chadocke he sent for me and I rid behind hime home. The remainder of this month to the 14th. May I was sadly efflicted with pains but the lord restored me.

May 14. 1666.

-14. Munday.

I went to Robert Rosbothoms and was all right.

-28. Munday.

Was the first day I could say I was well so that it pleased God to efflict me for 5 weekes just the last day of this month I was but weake and I went with Joshuah Naylor to whit leigh greene on purpose to recreate my selfe and Watts wife made much ove me. Mr. Sorowcolds man came for me att my comeing home I had a booke of Mr. Ambroses late minister of Preston who at the end of the booke had theses psalms in meeter.

Psalm 100.

All men of mortell birth
Yt dwell in all ye earth
O make a noise to God with Joys
and serve the lord with mirthe.
....

Psa 108 i part.
O God I fix my hart
My glory bears apart
And as my tongue so shall my songe
Praise thee with musicks art.

71

psal. 150.
Praise ye the lord most high
With his sanctuary
In topmost tower of his great power
With praise hime magnifie.

....

The psalms copied by the diarist are taken from the last page of the Media: The Middle Things, 4to. 1659 (page 576) and were put there for the purpose of provoking cheerefulness amongst Christians. They are not the composition of Ambrose, but are described as having been 'translated by Mr W.B.' It is noticable that in his book, which it appears Lowe was familiar, there is a section on commendation of the keeping of diaries - a matter which was then regarded as a characteristic of reflective Christians. The chapter is headed 'Of the time of Selfe-tryal' (i.e. self examination). After discussing the subject he adds; 'To this purpose were read of many ancients that were accustomed to keep Diaries of Day Books of their actions and out of them to take an acount of their lives. Such a Register of God's dealings towards him and his dealing towards God in main things the Lord put into a poor creature's heart (i.e. into his own heart) to keep in the year 1641, ever since which time he hath continued it, and once a year purposes by God's grace to examine himself by it. In his chapter on 'Experiences' (vi., and v, pages 176 seq), he advises that there should be three heads in a Diary for Experiences, Texts and Dispositions to be prayed for.

June 1666.

-i. Friday and Saturday.
        Both these day I was saddened in conditon in my thoughts by reason of the great debits but hope in in god that he will helpe me out.

-3. lords day.
        I went to Billinge Chappell to hear Mr. Blackeburne and he was glad to see me recovered he tooke me into Humphrey Cowlys and spent 6d on me and then I walked downe to Blackey hurst and so parted.

-8. Friday.
        I went to bringe John Jenkins wife old cock towarsd Winwick I intended to go to Winwick but I found myselfe unable and soe returned home.

-14. Thursdy.
        I went to Whitleige greene with John Potter and Thomas Harison and lost 2d att bowles and so came home.

-20th. Wedensday.

Att night I went to old John Robinsons and was there all night and widow Jackson promised me her horse to go to Chester.

-24. lords day.

I went att noone into Abram to Ann Taylors and Emme Potter was there but she would not adnitt me to speake to her soe I had Thomas Hesketh with me and we went to the Brinne and cald at Bein forlonge of younge Mr. Gerard and he accomodated us with drinke so returninge thanks we parted and came to Brinne to see some worke tooles that he had hid and so we came home.

-28. hursday.

I set forwards for Chester on widow Jaxon lent me her horse and near Fradsham bridge the horse halted exteminly I alighted of and puld single spike out of his foote nd the horse did a little halt I gat well to Chester by gods helpe went to Mr. Swift to whom I payd ten pound I lay att dragon I went to hear organs and the quiristers and I was wearie as I went in the midle of their service.

-29. friday.

I sat homewards haveing as I thought well done my busines and att Warrington I lighted and stayd awhile and so came home but with all... in the way Mr. John Potter ill tipled who I did not leave till I came home.

July 1666.

-i. lords day.

The scholemaster of Ashton came and intreated me to goe with hime to Standish to speake to Mr. Bowker to be his freind for the obtaininge of a schoole near Preston. I went with hime being bound in charities it raind notwithstandinge we went and when we came to Standish he was in one Thomas Smiths and he went for me we went to hime and att nine we dined with hime att Thomas Taylors in the Brickhouse and he promised to doe in the hime did lye.

-2. Munday.

Mr. Hopwood and his wife ware att John Jenkinsons and sent for me I went and spent me 4d. which was contrarie to Mr. Hopwood.

-3. tusady.

Emm Potter had ecquainted me that she was told that my brother bore me a bastard I conceived who had spoken it for to be Elizabeth Potter and she was att this present in towne so I sifted it out and found that she was the woman and she told me yt Will Morris had expressed it I resolved for Leigh and intended to be the death of Will and intended to call for my brother and have hime with me but I was prevented for I cald att Heapys and there was John Chodocke came by and Mr.

73

Holewist. I rid behind John Chadocke to Lowton Smithys and so came to Leigh Izibell Grundies cald for a chambr and sent for Will Morris he came and Thomas Rushworth with hime I wished hime to give place awhile when he was gone I to Will and buffeted hime very mery Nicholas Mathr came up and was very vehamant against me we parted that house and went to widow Ranicars I spent me 12d. so came and did lye with Clarke the other morninge I went to doe some business with my Mr. and I told hime my case and he was ill troubled att it and counceled me for my good so I came home with sad spirit and I cald of my brotherly Henry Haoughton and he was gone to be married so I parted.

-16. Munday.

I went with John Potter and Joshua Naylor to Henry Birchell to see a cock to fight I was ill troubled in my mind that I went.

-28. lords day.

I went to Wiggan on purpose to hear the Bishop for I was somwhat discomposed in mind by reason of Emm Potter and me fallinge out and I went to shake it out of me and I heard the Bishop he preached against atheisticalness.

August 1666.

-1. Wedensday.

I went to Neaton faire in the afternoone and met my Mr.

-5. lords day.

I went to Billinge chappell to hear Mr. Blakeburne I went in the afternoone.

-9th. thursday.

I went to Warrington and payd 52 shillings where I owd it up and downe.

-13.

I went to Wiggan but came too late to hear the Bishop preach.

-15

I went to Prescott being Wedensday and I went upon an idle occasion god forgive me.

-16.

I was pensive and sad all day by reason I had heard something of Emms unfaithfulness to me and it greeved me very sore.

-20 lords day.

I went to Wiggan to hear the Bishop preach I dined with John Naylor att Eles leighes there was buryd behind the great church door within the church one sarjant Lanchshaw he lived in Scowles.

-24th friday.

Being Bartholomew day I hired a horse and went with Thomas leech to Crosson Mr. Pilkington was parson and one Will Harys livd with hime and he oud I monys and we went to got it but found him not at home we found Thomas Naylor there and through him and his sons persuasion we went with them to Chorley it was the faire I was no sooner gotton into the Towne but I met with Robt Reynolds and when I was alight he said I went to see a show concerning the lifes of man from his infancie to his old age we pted and when I came to receive my horse I wanted a sha(?) all I spent was 2d so I came easily homewards and amidst Chorley moor I gat ashoo (a horseshoe) came homewards and in Wiggan Mr Bowker envited me to Ann Cason gave me a part of a bottle ot two of Rosbary ale and so I came home.

-31. thursday.

I went to Warrington and att my comeing home I was not well yet got home.

September 1666.

-2. lords day.

I went with John Potter to Wiggan to hear the bishop but he was gone to Knowsley and he had burned 4 or 5 bey of stabelinge and shipeninge this morninge by the carlesnes of the groome who let the candle burne att his beds head and he fell esleep.

-4. tusday night.

I went to old John Robinson was all night O how comfortable is the communion of saints.

-18. friday.

I went with John Potter to Winwicke and Mr. Potter envited me to dinner and att after prays for it was St. Mathews day he went with us into the Springe and we spent 4d and att night as we came home we overtooke Emm and Kenion together and I was ill troubled.

-19 Saturday.

I went to my brothers into Burtonwood and on lords day morninge we came for Ashton and cald to see Braidley Hall which I admird to se so godly a fabrick lying wast.

October 1666.

-13th friday.

I went with Raph Winstanley and John Potter to the funerall of old Mr. Bankes of Winstanley who was interred att Wiggan Mr. Blakeburne preached.

The Mr. Banks referred to would be William Banks of Winstanley Esq., son of James Banks Esq., who at his death would be about thirty two years of age.

-16. Monday.

Mr. Blakeburne wishd me to go with John Naylor and Will Chadocke to see what people would guie towards the reliefe of such needie psons as had sustained losse by the great fire in London and to set their names down which we did over the one halfe of Ashton.

> The Great Fire of London had broken out on the 2nd. September before and many old church registers and parish records contain references to public collections on behalf of the sufferers similar to that for which the Diarist canvassed half Ashton.

-29.

I went to Robert Rosbothome and was all night.

November 1666.

3d lords day

I went with John Potter to Winwicke and Mr. Potter envited me to Diner and I went.

-27. tusday.

I went to Leigh and made all things streight with my Mr and turned over John Greenhough and Thomas Greenhough to discharge the debt I owd which my Mr assented to. He would have faine concluded me with the debt but I would not so he tooke Thomas Greenoughs bond with his son John Greenhoughs bond for all the debt I owd to him so he cleard me before John Chadocke in his own shope and before John Greenhough who came with me home and att Joshua Naylors spent either 6d.

-30. friday. St Andrews day.

I went to Garswood about widow Taylors busines of exchangeinge the leas and Sr William made a promise .... the was between hall and kitchen that he would speake to his sonn for it was he that must do that busines.

December 1666.

-2 lords day.

John Potter and I went to Billinge Chappell Mr. Blakeburne preached. It was a cold day and att noone Humphry Cowlys house was so thronged that we could not attain a fire to sit by but we sacriciced ourselves ore twopenny flagon in a cold chamber att noone there was Henry Birchall with us the younger we had each of us a messe a pottage we spent 3d. a peece.

-15. Saturday.

I went to the doelfull funerall the reverand Mr. John Blakeburne at Winwicke Mr. Potter preached in a very pethaticall manner out of the 14 Revelations i part of the 13 verse blessed are the dead that due in the Lord; he in the close of his sermon spoke excellentie truely tho mournfullie in comendation of Mr. John and indeed the neighbourhood sustaone great losse by death.

> The Winwick registers contain the coroberative entry.- '1666, Dec. 15 Mr. John Blakeborne, of Blackey Hurst.'

-16. lords day.

I went to the funerall of Ann Taylor who was married to Raph Ashton in Abram and I went fastinge from home so att noone when we had buried the Corps and expected according to custome to have some refreshment and ware a companie of neighbours sate togather round about a table as John Potter Tho Harrison and others the Dr. comes and prohibits the filling of any drinke till after prayrs so I came home with Thomas Harrison and we expected to have cald at Neawton but here we ware disapointed but att last with nuch vexation I gat to Ashton with a hungery belly and honest Thomas Harrison and right true harted Ellin the hastie yet all love did much refresh my hungry pallet with a big cup full an after that half full againe of goo pattage.

-11. tusday.

I went to Leigh and gat my bonde in from my Mr.

-21. friday night.

I went into old William Hasledens in Ashton his wife was sicke and I read in the practice of pitie as I went reading she gave up the ghost.

-23. lords day.

I went to Wigan being much disconsulate yet the Lord incouraged me for my hope is in hime.

-27.

Old Thomas Harison was come over out of Halsall and his sone and others amongst whome I was one went to Jenkins to drinke and Mr Hopwood had seen a letter out of Ouldham to envite me with John Jenkins to his house and John moved me to goe soe I was resolved to goe forthwith that night and it was showry snowy night but indeed the maine reason that nmoved me to goe this night was because Emm was gone to Chadocke Hall whome I intended to see but could not soe we came to Manchester about 3 or 4 o'clock and with much adoe gat a fire in Ffennall streete at one Humphrey Pecockes where we stayd till paryers in the church and then we went to morninge prayr when it was done we went into a little old womans house att goeing out of the church and we boughte a pudding for 1d. and a loafe 1d. and eate part and gave rest to old woman and so patrted to Ouldham where we stayed till munday and then came home away by Midleton and over Walkedon moore where we came much discontented but with nuch trouble of mind and weariness of body we came home.

Walkden Moor at the time Roger Lowe crossed it in winter was an inhospitable district. The Eccles Register for about this date contains an entry of the burial of a man who had perished in crossing it.

Jenuery 1666.

-2. Wedensday.

I went to funerall of younge John Potter of Lilly Lane to Winwicke.

-6. Lords day.

Mr. Swift was come to Leigh and sent for me I oud hime 9li. and had no mony to pay time and I was troubled but it pleased god that I gat 3li. in readiness forthwith I blesse god and it gave good content I was at night with John Chadock and supd with my Mr.

-24. thursday.

I went to Warrington and payd some debts I there owd and att my comeinge home was wellcomed with the news of John Greenhoughs running away which was no little trouble to me for I looked upon myselfe even as blasted in the bud unles the lord be my help who hath helped me hitherto and surlie will not now forsake me for my expectations is from hime 3li.

ffebruary 1666.

-2. Saturday morneinge.

Thomas Parkinson came to me to write a letter for his wife for he had been under the execution of a warrant and was gotton for his attendencers.

-3. lords day.

I went with John Potter and Tho Harrison to fatch their wives home from Holland I was nott att this time mery for I could not becaus I lay under sad

78

reproaches of persequuteing tongues such as The Naylor Glasier Joshua Naylor and Mary Rogrson about the debt of John Greenhough but I trust in God for aid he is my refuge the hinieneus and Philetus and Alexandr as copersmiths if not worse have done me much evill the lord reward them.

-5. tusday.

    I went to Wigan to Mr. Jolley who was sloe exers for a John Greenough and I movd hime for me but before I intreated Mr. Earle curate for his assistance and I told home all my mind I came hme better satisfied a greate deale.

-6. Wedensday.

    my Mr came to Ashton and some writeings I had to seale we ware seald between hime and Raph.

-Wednesady.

    I received that sad sorrowfull newes of Mr. Woods death upon the

The diary here unfortunately is imperfect. The last entry is crossed through, and the remainder of the page is free from any entries excepting the lines as follows:-

Its Gods yt fixt my love on onely one
Whom Ill love till I dye or dye a Nunn.

The Rev .James Woods has been before referred to. In the obituary at the end of the Diary, the old Puritan minister is given as 10th .February 1666-7 and this would make the entry in the date of the Diary to be about the 13th. the Rev. James Woods was buried at Grappenhall near Thewall where he resided after leaving Ashton. The Grappenhall registers contain the following entries relating to Mr. Woods and his wife:- 1666-7 Feb. 12. Buried Mr. James Woods of Thelwall minister.' '1668-9 Jan .12. Buried Mrs. Alice wife of Mr. James Wood of Thelwall.'

March 1667.

-28. thursday.

    I went with Constable to Ashton to helpe to gather Pole mony I was att this time in a sad sorowfull Estate by reason of my fear of povertie but o my soule cast they burden upon the lord he will sustaine thee meny be ye miserys of ye rightous but the lord will delivr dos no X call .. come unto me all yee yt are weary and I will give you rest. Indeed I must confess I have a proud envicus spirit and thinking of othrs ... and am apt to censure god for hard measure unto me yet grudge not to see wicked men prosperus its but awhile they shall flourish thus prosperitie will be hard peniworthe for ym waite thou on gd o my soule and keape his way o labour to be content with thy prsant condition gd sees it good it should soe be o do thou so too labour O my soule to bringe thy desires to thy condition not thy condition to thy desires.

-30 lords day.

I went to Winwick with John Potter and dined att Mr. Potters house.

April 1667.

-1.

I went this morninge to Warrington to buy commodities.

-7. lords day.

I went to Sarah Hasleden to Wiggan and heard Bishop...

-8. Monday.

I was sent for to Leigh by my Mr. who had a child interred on this day Raph Hasleden lent me a horse.

This entry mey give a clue to the name of Roger Lowe's master, the Leigh tradesman, who is so often referred to but never by name. In July 25th. 1663 the Diarist says he was in Leigh at 'our child's christening, he was named Edward.' Roger Lowe no doubt was speaking of one of his master's children as on the 13th. of the same month he records his 'dames' confinement. In the Leigh register no christenings are entered on the 25th. but Edward, son of Thomas Hamond de Westleigh was baptized on the following day- the 26th. The interment of the child mentioned in the above entry took place between the 7th. and the 14th. March, 1667, fort he date and day prefixed to the entry is indistinct in the Diary though it appears to be the 8th., on which day the Leigh registers contain the entry of the babtism of Martha, daughter of Thomas Hamond de Westleigh. The inference is very probable that a mistake had been made in either the Diary or the church records.

-14. saturday.

I was sadly unfavoured in my thoughts this morninge through fear of world and therefore took pen in hand and made these verses followinge.
The greifes are many i'th world I far see
Ah Lord when wilst thou come to pitie poore me
I'me soe best with greiges I cannot tell
Not know how to live i'th world nor where to dwell
But this I'me sure my hope is fixt in thee.
And this joyes me in greatest extremitie
Thou wilt not suffer me long to live in woe.
Sure lord thoule come to visit the poor Low
Amen even soe lord Jesus in mercie
And not in Justice to me thy servant.

-22. lords day.

I went with Thomas Smyth and litle John Smith to hear Mr. Gregge who preacht att John Suttons and when we were at Parbridge by reason it was rainey we went to hear Mr. Aspinall it was nearer and we all runn home very wett but John Smith had lost Gloves and turned againe from Parr Hall and found them.

-23. Munday night.

I went to John Robbinsons and was all night safter this time I was sadly troubled in my thoughts but the lord is my suport.

-29th. lords day.

I went to hear Mr. Gregge preach att William Turner in Par att afternoone I came home and there was some Leigh persons att Chappell and I ingaged them into Tankerfields where I spent 6d but aftre theire parteinge a sad disaster befall me viz a fallinge out betweene Henry Kenion and me the after days I made it the lamentaion of my private thoughts.

May 1667.

-1. Wedensday.

Henry Kenion came to Tankerfields and sent for me and we ware both reconciled and I was som what joyful.

-2. thursday.

I went to Warington and payed some mony I there owd as I came home I intended to call on Mr. Potter meerly out of love but he would goe to take part of 2d in beere but seemd as if he ware angry which troubled me very sore. I came home very pensive and sad and not very well.

Mr. Thomas Potter so often refferred to in the diary was curate of Winwick and his burial is thus entered in the Winwick registers: '1671 Nov. 12 buried Mr. Thomas Potter, curate.'

-17. friday.

I went to Warington and sold Josephus a booke soe cald concerninge Jewish warrs I was att this time partly ingaged to go to Mr. Harwood who lived in Shrows bury to live with hime and he had ingaged one Edw Bowker de Warington to enquire of my disposition it troubled me sore.

Roger Lowe is evidently in business difficulties. The later portion of his diary contains frequent references to his unfortunate want of success as an independent shopkeeper and his determination to give up business and return to his old position as a servant.

81

19.- lords day.

I went with William Knowles William Hasleden and others into Windle to Cowly Hill to Mrs. Harpers house and hear Mr Gregge preach out of these words try all thinges but hold all fast that which is good.

June 1667.

-2. lords day.

I wemt to Wiggin and dined att James Asltleys for he would have to diner.

-9. lords day.

I went to one Tickles house in Sutton with William Knowle and litle John Smith and heard Mr. Gregge out of these words be ware yee of the leaven of the pharisees which is hipocresie.

-23. lords day.

I sat forward with James Jenkins for Chester faire and when I came there I was scarcely well yet it pleased god to inable me so as I did my busines very well.

-25th. Tuesday.

I came home.

-28. friday.

I went with William Naylor to Crosson to Mr. Pilkingtons man who had owd me Mr. 3s but I could not get it. Emma Potter and Eles Taylor was att Halsall therfore I hastened thither on the

-29th day Saturday.

which was 8 miles come to Halsall and send for them and they stayd rather too longe that I went myselfe to old Thomas Harisons who made much for me and constrained me to stay all night and we went all together to the alehouse and ware mery and the next day I came home.

July 1667.

-9. lords day.

I went to James Lowes in Neawton Comon where Mr. Baldwin preacht.

-10. Munday.

I went to Warington faure and mett Mr. Swift.

-15. Munday.

I went to Halsall for to fatch Eles Taylor home but she could not come with me, soe I lost my labour. Att Ormeskirke I stayd and spent 2d and went into church and look'd in Earle Darbyes Tombe and we came home onely I cald att Holland att one Corles house and gave my horse 4d in ale.

The Derby chapel and vault in Ormskirk Church were constructed by Edward the third Earl of Derby. The last Stanley buried in the vault when the diarist visited Ormskirk was the seventh Earl, whose execution in Bolton in October, 1651, must have taken place within the recollection of Roger Lowe.

-18. thursday.

I went to Prescott for to receive 5li. 10s. of John Walls for Henry ffeildinge but received none. I came away by my brothers who lived att one Traves house near Windleshey Chappell sayd diner and soe came home and att the yate that enters into the further end of town field comeing from Dock lane I found a shoo with a silver clasp in the highway.

-20. Saturday.

I went to Halsall to fatch home Elles Taylor and mett her at Ormeskirke.

-28. Munday.

I went to Warrington in compenie with John Potter to Winwick who was exceedinglie troubled with tooth ache and James Corles in pullinge it out broke it. Att comeinge home from Warington I went to Mr. Potters and John Potter was laid down soe I went to the schoole and Mr. Jones and I went to the springe and sent for John Potter who came as we came home we cald att Heapies and there had hott rye loaf and butter and I had some sugr and nutmeg given me att Warington. I would have a flaggon burnt for John and had.

Mr. Jones was master of Winwick Grammar School and succeeded Ralph Gorse M.A. who is stated by Mr. Beamont to have left Winwick to take the headmastership of Macclesfield School in 1667. In the entry for 6th. February, 1668-9, Mr. Jones is distinctly called 'Winwick schoolmaster.' The name must be added to the list of the masters of this school solely on the evidence of the diary.

-29. tusday.

I went to the funerall of Thomas Leech inkeaper.

August 1667.

-2. tusday.

I went to Neawton faire and to the race with John Potter but stayd not longe nor was not very long.

The confirmation to the barons of Newton of an early charter obtained in the 29th. Ed. I (1300), expressly granted three days' faires on the eves, days and morrows of St. John ante portam Latinan (6th. May) and St. Germanus the Confessor (31st. July). The diarist is very careless in these dates but the autumn fair which he attended was evidently held on or about the proper charter day. The later Newton faire is now held on the 11th. August the result of the change of style in the last century the originally day and not the date having been almost supersticiously respected by the country people.

4. lords day.

I went with John Jenkins to Standishe Church and heard Mr. Bowker preach and dined att home.

-6. Tusday.

I went with William Hasleden to Wiggan to speake to Mr. Earle to mary hime.

-15. Thursday.

I went to Mr. Walls in Prescott but did not gat no monys.

-18. lords day.

I went to see Tom Birchall who was sicke.

-27. tusday.

I went to Prescott againe to Mr. Walls but he was not at home.

September 1667.

-8. Munday.

I went to Winwicke to Mrs. Potters funerall and Elizabeth Taylor rid behind me.

The burial of the wife of the curate of Winwick is recorded in the Winwick registers but the date given is two days later than that of the diarist: '1667, Sept. 10 buried Margaret, vx. of Mr Thomas Potter curate.'

-10 Wedensday.

I went to Warrington. John Plumpton tooke his leave of Ashton this day and I fled with hime att Warrington bridge very dolefully Thomas Peake would gladly hire me.

-13 ffriday.

I went to Precott to Mr. Walls John Hampson went with me and about one and the same occasion but he would not be seene.

-18. Wedensday.

I went to Warington and I promisd Peake to serve hime for three years for 20li.

-22. lords day.

I went to Wigan haveing no occasion but meeley to put of a troubled mind.

-23. Munday.

According to my promise I went to Warington to meet Tho. Peake.

-29. lords day.

I went to John Robinson and was all night for they lent me a horse to Chester faire a very rugged night it was. The other morninge I hastened way and it was a very tempestuous morneinge and in Warrington George Chapman gave me 2d. in ale and behind ffradsham Hamond overtooke me I gat to Chester and payd Londoners for my intentions was to buy nothinge and I went to the castle to see a man condemned a pretie young man he was and very sorie I was I gave a man 2d. in ale to let me admittance into castle yard and he tooke me up and downe. The souldiers was most of them all drunke and glad I was when I was gotton out of hegates from amongst them.

October 1667.

-1. Tusday.

I came home I blesse God very well but it was a very stromie and ranie day.

-28.

I quitted my selfe of all shop effaires in Ashton and resigned then over to Thomas Hamond and I ingaged myself to Thomas Peake service and after I came to him I found his wife of soe cross a disposition that it put me in a troubled condition and occasioned me to write these verses followinge:-

In to wt strange ragion am I posted now
Soe hott a climate as I know not howe
To enjoy my selfe much more to live in peace
Unles Jehovah move their tongues to cease
The lord of hosts yt rules in heaven high
Looke downe and help thy servt mightily
Show me such favour as the world may know.
Yt thou esteemeth of thy servant Lowe
Yt such as have no reason nor yet faith
May learne to live in peace and not in wrath
Lord if thou please to show thyselfe my friend.
I matter this would for to offend
My Saviour dead (in griefes) ile come to thee
Theres safe protection in necessitie.
I live in griefes I know not where to goe
I come to thee (lord shelter thy poor Lowe)
Deliverance I hope will come ere long
And I shall saye not longe the mourners song
Providence sees it good I tossd should be
Upon the waves of wordly miserie
And tho I be thus fettered in the worlds greife
Providence will at last yeild me reliefe
And this I me sure faults have ceased this
(Require then not) God doth nothing amisse.
My soul frett not be patient but awhile
Yt face now frownes will ere longe on thee smile
And though he suffer thee in Kedar to dwell
Amongst such blacke mouthes as doe yawn like hell
Yet be assured god will preserve thee soe
(They may thee scare) they shall not hurt poor Lowe
Trust then in god heele comfort thee in touble
And answer all thy grieves with care joyes double
Waite on the lord live up right in gods way
Heele recue out of greives heele not longe stay
Take patiantly the worlds affronts (for why)
Because it loves its owne nine will deny
Aprove thyselfe a stranger to the worlds friends
For heaven att last to such will make amends

I had made a piece of promse to stay three yeares with Mr. peake but I found his wife
of such a pestilentiall nature that I was weary in a few weakes in december it pleased
God sorely to visit me with a sad affliction and longe for the space of nine weeks after
which it pleased god to recover me and I went againe to Mr. Peakes after many
envitations: in which time I sent to Emme my designes and thoughts enclosed in a

letter and in short time made a conclusion of my overtyred thoughts and upon the 23rd. of March, 1667-8 we consumates out grand desire of marriage att Warrington done br Mr. Ward minister of Warrington att my cozen Beckinson house William Eccleston was my good friend I brought Emme to Neawton and shee was turned off from her sister and knew not where to Lodge all night it was her pleasur that I should turn back againe to Warrington which I did with William Eccleston and Henry Heckinbothom who accompanied us to Neawton.

(The diary breaks off here)

The above entry confirms the supposition that the master to whom the diarist was apprenticed was Thomas Hanmond de Westleigh. Roger Lowe records that the business was the one he originally managed for his master and which the latter turned over to him. The business not prospering it is evident that the diarist resigned it back to his master and returned to service as a shopman.

ffebruarie 1668-9.

-i. Munday.
      I did nothing but stayd att home but was angered in my mind att Martha Knowle who had undermined me and gotten a booke out my hands.

-2. tusday.
      I went with Thomas Harison at Halsall to seale 2 indentures betwixt Thomas Harrison and Thomas Neale his prentice I went before Thomas and att Ormeschurch I staid in hime we ytayd until Thursday and soe came home.

-6. saturday.
      William Eccleston came into towne and he gave me a quart of ale and enjoined me to goe the lords day following to Broad oake and gave Mr. Haryes daughter a note this day Mr. Jones Winwick schoole master sent for me to come to Winwicke upon Monday following for his patron Mr. Leegh would come and he would make a speech.

Mr. Jones's patron 'Mr Leigh' was Piers Legh Esq. of Lyme. Winwick Grammar Schoole was founded about 1553 by Gowther Legh, son of Sir Peter Legh, knight and priest whose monumental brass is still to be seen in Winwick Church. Sir Peter Legh, knight, grand nephew of Gowther, built the schoolhouse in 1618.

-7. lords day.
      I went to broad oake Mr Gregg preached out 2 Philip 9,10.

I went to Winwicke and heard Mr. Jones make his speech to Mr. Leegh I went to Hall Winwick and dind there after I came to with Mr Watt to the Clarkes house and Cez Potter had given Mr. Watt 1d. to spend and I laid another 2d to it and when that was drinke I parted.

-9. tusday.

Richard Orme came to Ashton and I was with John Potter and hime late in Ale house which lord forgive.

-10 Wedensday.

I went to Nicholas Crofts to get in a debt but gat nothing.

-11 Thursday.

I went to Senelly Greene to get a debt oweinge me by Mr Gerard Schoolemaster att my returne home I mett with Mr. James Woods comeing out of his unkles Raph Lowes so he asked me to goe with them to the Alehouse and I went with Tom Hasledens and Mr. Woods was hartie and healthfull I spent 2d.
(A whole page of the diary is left blank here).

-5. lords day.

I received some piece of disgrace in the chappell from Mr. Atkinson by reason I did not with others stand up at the readinge of the Gospell but as to the publicke it was little noted but I took it heinously in my one thoughts by reason I had bespoke my thoughts to hime befor that I could not conforme to any such formes but att after eveinge prayr I went to himme att Elline Ashton and I told hime my mind to the full that standing att Gospell with other ceremonies now in use was a meere Romish foperie and I should never doe it but sith I could not come to the publick ordinances without publik disturbance for a ceronoiall failinge I should thenceforward betake my selfe to such recepticles where I could to my poor abilitie serve god without disturbance. Ralph Winstanley Atkinsons disciplin of the Blacke tribe of Gad came in and spoke his venome in a very arogant manner but I flie to god for refuge.

'J.E.B' says in the Manchester Courier notes that '"he piece of disgrace' which Roger received at Ashton Chapel for not standing up at the reading of the Gospel perhaps took the form of a public reproof from the minister, Mr. Atkinson. Roger had stated his view of the matter. There appears to be no rubric in the Prayer book urging a standing posture; but it was named in the Scotch Prayer Book. The custom was however already established in the time of Chrysostom; and it was adopted in England. (See Campion and Beamont's Interleaved Prayer Book, pp. 83, 85). Bp. Buckeridge in a sermon 1618 has the remark that it was the customary to stand at the Creed and reading of the Gospel and to sit at the reading of the Psalms and Chapters. The matter before the Civil War formed a subject of enquiry in the Bishop's Visitations one of

Bishop William's questions being whether the Minister 'called upon' the people to stand at any other time than at the Creed and Gospel. On the other had in the London Petition against Bishops 1640 standing up at Gloria Patri; and at the reading of the Gospel was enumerated among some of the Bishop's innovations; and Prynne made the same complaint in regard to Hereford Cathedral.

-16. Munday.

I went to Edge greene to get some money owing to me by Nicholas Crouker but get none cald att Tho Whitle tooke a pipe of Tob. and then went and bought off Cooper some Ash wood to be two cheares and brought a peece home with me.

-18. Wedensday.

Emme and I went to Warrington and bought soem odd things and came home and was in night it was very stormie night John Lowe Blacksmith let her ride behind hime.

-25, thursday.

I went to Winwicke to the funeral of Dicke Lands Mr. Potter preached out of 10 Job 20 verse.

March 1668.

- Munday.

I went to John Lowes Smithie to get some odd things made. I went to old John Robbinson to bespeake John Marshes thoughts to Widow Jaxon old Johns daughter being desired by John Marsh and shee consented he should come thursday cum seavenight after.

-7 lords day.

I went to my cozen Robert Rosbothom and heard Mr. Baldwin preach out of Rom 25 26 verses.

-11. thursday

Honest Mr. Hayhurst came to Towne to sec me and I was glad to see him.

-14. lords day.

I went to Leigh to bid farewell to poor Mr. Braidley Hayhurst Mr. Lever preacht out 14 pro 9 verse att my comeinge home I cald on my sister Katherin and advised her for her good to bethinke herselfe and live godly consideringe she had but a short time to live here but she was highly offended so I came home being late in the night.

Of Mr. .Bradley (or Braydley as he often writes himself) Hayhurst's early life much is not known. He was Presbyterian minister of Leigh Parish Church during the Commonwealth. His name as 'preacher of the word' at Leigh is suscribed to the 'Harmonious Consent' of the Ministers of Lancashire. After his ejection after the Act of Unifornmity he was presented to Taxal Church in Cheshire (on the borders od Derbyshire), by Edmund and Reginald Downes where however he appears to have remained for aboutt two years only. We next meet with him for about 1670 when he was presented to Macclesfield Church and it is probable that on his taking of this living that Roger Lowe records his leave taking in Ashton in March, 1669. He remained in Macclesfield for 10 to 12 years and is said to have died in 1682-3 but there is no entry of his burial in the Macclesfield registers. His connection with Macclesfield ceased and he may possibly have died at or near Ashton or Winwick.

-18. friday.

I went to the funerall of Ellin Potter daughter to Thomas Potter and was interred at Winwick as we came into Winwick Church yard Captain Risleys soldiers are in training and when we ware att prayrs in the church upon the funeralls occasion the shouldiers discharged the musquests three times.

There were two Risleys living at the time either of whom might have been the captain. John Risley, of Risley, Esquire who was buried at Winwick 19 July, 1682 and John Risley his son and heir apparent who was buried at Winwick as John son of John Risley Esq. 30th. March, 1676. The latter was the father of Captan John Risley, of Risley, (born 1675 and died 1702) the last of that family.

-20. Saturday.

I went to Winwick schoole to get Mr. Jones to pay me 30s. but gat none. This evening old Thomas Harison was come over and I spent 2d.

-21. lords day.

I went to Laverpool was all night att my brothers and the next day went forward to Liverpoole payd Mr. Johnson 5li. I owd him

-22 day

Came home -1669

-27. Saturday.

I went to Leigh bought of my Mr. 9 yard and a half of Cersie for a suite of clothes for myselfe.

-29. Munday.

I went to Warington and Mrs. Peake had laid a lye on me about their debts which occasioned some griefe but I cleared myself to her shame.

-12. March 1673-4

I went to Coz Robt Rosbothom to Rixham faire to seeke his mare yt was stolen over night & we met with Mathew Cooke who we conjectured to be ye theefe & upon our wordes he fled and left a stolen mare we securd in towne & was afterwards owned.

[THE DIARY ENDS HERE.]

AN ACCOUNT OF THE SEAVERAL NAMES AND PSONS THAT ARE DEAD IN ASHTON AND BURYED ATT WINWICKE 1671.

Impr May 1671.

-iith. Thursday. William Watt son of Will Watt dyed of the pockes was a child interred att Winwicke.

-8. Munday. Eles uxor Robt Worthington dyd in child bed.

-19. friday. dyed John Plumpton, Crooke backt, he dyed in the outhouseing of John Jenkinson.

-15. Munday. Margret the daughtr of James Thomason maryd to Rigbie of ye yate in Houghton dyd and was buryd att Deane

June 1671.

-i. ffriday. died Eles the daughter of William Hasleden of Whitleig green Locksmith.

July 1671.

-i. Saturday eveninge. dyed old Jane Rigbie and was buryd the other day att Wiggan.

-8. lords day. Edmond the sonn of Adam Gaskell, lyes near Dr. Cloughs.

August 1671.

-10. Thursday a child Nicholas Crofts lyes at Ashton chappell.

-25. Wedensday. Marye the daughter of Lin Knowles lyes at Winwicke.

-23. August. a child of Henry Houghton of Hadock was nursed with ff... Lowe lyes att Chappell.

-28. Tusday. a wench of James Haselden de Claddin Hey and buried at Winwick.

September 1671.

-5. Tusday. a younge women sister to Henry Naylor being lame and a child of Gilbert Cooke son buryd att Winwicke.

October 1671.

-16 Munday a child of Dr. Cloughes interred Winwicke.

-17. Tusday. Thomas Kellitt lyes at Ashton chapell.

-20. Friday. this afternoone dyd Eles Manchester of ... and on Saturday wrs buryd att Winwicke; about this time a child of William Hopes interred att Ashton..

November 1671.

ii Saturday. between the hours of 4 & 5 in the morninge dyed Mr. Potter vicar of Winwicke, he heard Tho. Gifford passing peale on his dyeing bed and askd who was dead, and he lived about half an hour after. He was buryd on the lord's day in the chancell att noone and his wifes coffin was bared all over and he laid top of her.

As already mentioned in a previous note Mr. Potter was curate of Winwick, and not the vicar.

-27. Wedensday a son of Richard Cloughes interred att Winwicke.
December 1671.
-12th. a child of Robert Worthington that the wife dyd of befor and it was buryd att Winwicke.
-14. Thursday in the morneinge Adam Gaskell that lives ovr against Dr. Cloughes hanged himselfe but the reason is not yet knowen onely there is a comon report that the Inhabiters of Bitter Hootes Estate are haunted by spirits. but the rather is to be beleeved is that Mr. Banks of Winstanley deprived him of his inheritence he was heir to. He was buryed at Ashton Chappell. A child of Edw. Dusworth buryd att Winwick.
-15. Friday. about 7 & 8 of the clock in the eveninge dyed Robert Pendleberry cald Marquess and was buried on Munday the 18th. day at Winwicke.
-19. Tuesday. the wife of Tho Hart dyd in childbed and was buryd att Ashton Chappell.
-23. Saturday. about the hour of 9 a clock in the ... dyed John Hasleden a very old man borne ... house att the mill in Goleborne was ... on Sunday the 24th at Winwick.

Jenuery 1671.

-i. Munday dyed Tho Litler and old ... was interred att Winwicke.
ffebruery 1671.
-5. Munday. dyed a child of ... he was a lad and interred ....
-6. Tusday. dyed old George ... and was iterred at ....
A Bastard child of Ellin C.
-7. Wedensday evening. dyed old Eles Harsh wife to old John Hash Blindman of Whithip greene, & was interred att Winwick.
-9. Friday. a child of James Winstanley lives att old Lowbrooks was interred at Winwick.
Also about 3 of the clock this evening dyed William Berchall als Crossman he maryd the younger daughtr of Edward Clarke and he was interred at Winwick on Saturday the 10 h of this Februery.

-ii. Munday. dyed Wiliam Darbishire he liv'd and ... out of Mr. Landrs house in Windy banke lane ... interred at Winwick the 12th day.
-. .... dyed Elizabeth the wife of Georg Low ... land was interred at Winwick.
-. .... died Ellin the wife of Robert Green Legh ... of a Dropsie was buryd .... att Winwick.

March 1671-72.

-26. Tusday. dyed a child basely gotton of the bodie of Katherin Shaylor & fatherd upon Thomas Greenhogh & was interred at Chappell it was a wench.
-28. thursday night about ten of the clock deyd Izibell the wife of Henry Berchall of Teand brend was interred the 29th att Winwick.

April 1672.

-16. Wednesday. dyed Thomas sonn of John Knowles mason was interred at Winwick.
-16. Wedensday in ye afternoon dyed Anne the wife of Robert Downall was interred att Winwick.
-18. Friday. dyed Mary the mother of Thomas Gererd of Hollin Hey was interred the 19 att Winwick.
-20 Saturday. dyed Susan the wife of Samuell Darbishire and was buried on Sunday the 21th of Aprill att Holland She came to John Darbyshires, Sammuell her husbands ffathers, on pleasure and was there deliverd of a child and was visited with a distemper cald Creaze and of it dyed.
-25. dyed William the son of Samuell Darbyshire was interred at Holland the ffriday being 26th day that day fortnight he was borne that same day fortnight and was buryid.
-29. Munday. A Bastard child of Jane Cronchleyes who is now att house of correction dyed and was nursed with John Howes wife cald Frims and was interres att Chappell it was a man child.
in all 43.

May 1672.

-3. Thursday. dyed Ellin the wife of John Robinson was above 80 yeares of age was interred the 5th being Saturday att Ashton chappell.
-6. Munday. dyed Humphrey Markland at Locker and was interred the other day att Winwicke.
-12. lords day.
     James Abram who was a caterer to the preists att Brinne went and Bathed in the midle Dame as we goe ore the head of to Wigan and was drowned

between 2 and 3 of Clock. I was by when they took him out of water which was with trusting a pikill into his body and so lifted hime up and dragged hime to the side per Tho. Worthington.

June 1672.

-4. Tusday. In the afternoone dyed James Turton.
-12. Wedensday. was killd a lad cald Benchall he was drawing coles in lower lane and a coale fell on his neck and so kild him, buryd att Ashton Chappell.

> This and other entries shew that too common cause of pit accidents, that known by colliers as 'fall of dirt' was two centuries ago one of the dangers of mining in Lancashire, although little coal was then raised and the mineral wealth of the county was scarcely known of. Until the reign of Henry III. the great coal mines of Lancashire were undisturbed and their full extent was not realised until the last century, when the agency of steam was practicaly applied to machinery, and deep mining was rendered possible and remunerative.

-25. June. dyed Margaret Benchall, sister to King the shoomakr was interred at Winwick.

July 1672.

-3. Wedensday. dyed Richard Ashton oditor of cole-pitt dyd about 8 of the clock in the morneinge buryed att Winwicke.
-9th. Tusday. This morneinge about 7 of the clock dyed Mary Wallis daughter to John Wallis in towne to the great greife and lamentation of the neighbourhood, was interred theday after att Winwick.
-10. Wednesday. dyed from Ince hall Mr John Gerard, Sr. William Gerard his youngest sonne, he was marryd to Mr. Gerard daughter if Ince Hall and there dyed and the day after Esqr. Gerard his eldest brother causd him to be fatched in the bottom of relune (?) and brought to Winwick and he was interred in the tombe under the great stone in Sr. William his chappell.
-13 Saturday. Before day died a child of John Shames in towne.

> The Gerards of Brynn are an old Lancashire Roman Catholic Family, the present representative being Lord Gerard, of Garswood Hall, raised to the peerage by the present government in 1875, formerly Sir Robert Tolver Gerard, Baronet. The barronage was conferred on Sir Thomas Gerard in the 9th James I. The ancient family of the Gerards is descended from Walter Fitzother, castellan of Windsor, in the time of William the Conqueror. William, the eldest son of William Fotzother took the name from Windsor and was ancestor to the Lords of Windsor and from the younger son of William Gerard, brother of

William the Gerards of Brynn are literally descended. (Baines) Several of the Gerards are buried at Winwick where the chapel on the north side of the nave of the church is the old chapel of the family.

-20. Saturday evenginge. dyed one Ffrancis sister to Henry Ffrance she dyd from Richard Weinwrights house on whitledge green she was a widow to a man that formerly made glasse in Pemberton & was interred att Ashton chappell.

-28. Lords Day night. dyed John Ffletcher wife was interred the 30th att Wincwicke being tuesday.

August 1672.

-3. Saturday. dyed Robert son & haire to Devid Pendleberie was interred the lords day after att Winwick.

-16 Friday. dyed Anne Ashton drivrs wife was interrd att Wigan.

-19 Munday night. dyed a litle child being a wench of Mathew Chadocks was buryd at Chappell.

September 1672.

-6. Friday. dyed Jane the wife of Thomas Harrison she was Lyths godsdaughter was interred att Winwick on Saturday.

-14. Saturday. was buryed att Ashton Chappell a basterd wench cald Crouchley.

-29. lords day. was buryd att Chappell a still borne child of John Ralphes.

October 1672.

-15. Tuesday. was interred att Ashton Chappell a child of Charles Gerards.

-21. Munday. dyed Margaret Berchall daughter to Tho Kinge was interred at Chappell.

November 1672.

-20. thursday. dyed old Izabel Chadocke.

-21. friday. A still borne child of Jeffry Berchall. Another child was also borne at this time who alsoe dyed and ware both buryd a child of Bead bowrs was buryd at Ashton Chappell.

December 1672

-3 tusday. was buryd att Winwick Thomas Houghton bitter footes sonne.
-8. lords day dyed Joince the wife of Henry Bankes.
-15. lords day. John Lowe cald white knight, dyed.-23. Munday. dyed Joh Clough the youngest sonne to Dr. Jarvis Clough.
-31. dyed a wench basely begotten of the body of Anne Gerard cald Buckestones.

Jenuery 1672.

-18. Saturday. about midnight dyed William Knowles barley man.
-21. Munday. was buryd on which day my little John was christened.
-21. Munday dyd Josiah Madoike a lusty young man Aprentice to Tho Collands.
Ffebruery 1672.
-15. Saturday. dyed old Richard Worthington out of Park Lane who had lived a longe time in extreame paine.
-19. Wednesday. about midnight died old William Marsh was interred Frfiday the 21st att Winkwick.

March 1672.

-1. Saturday. died Elizabeth the wife of George Allins, binge his 4th wife; she died about midnight.
-7. friday night. dyed Capt. Sorrowcold an old Cannibell, yt hath orethrowne many families, but hath now arrived att his one place, abundance of gold and silver was found under his hands.
Of the family of Sorrowcoals little is known. The burial is recorded in the Winwck register under the date of March 10th., as 'Mr. John Sorrowcold.'
-9. Lords day. died a child of Rogr Naylor junr a young Papist.
-13. dyed a daughter of John Leyland buryd att Chappell.
-17. Munday. dyed Thomas Gaskell calld sparse was buryd att Chappell.

April 1673.

-1. tuesday. dyed Anne Gerard daughter to Will Gerard als Manchester aged 5 weeks.
-9. Wednesday night. dyed a child of Will Cromptons.
-12. Saturday. dyed Tho, Darbshire an Apprentice to John Low blakesmith and son to Will Darbishire, Naylor.
-27. lords daynight. dyed William Ashton of the Crosse. was buryd on tursday after at Winwicke.
-29. Tusday. was buryed att Chappell a child of Ned Pooles. at same time dyed James Lowe lived in Lower lane a collier.

from 1 May 1672 to 1 May 1673 are dead and buryed within Ashton quarter in all 44.

May 1673.

-18. lords day morneing. was found dead in the bed a chiuld of Henry Lowes cald Gib catt.
-25. lords day. in the afternoone dyed Symon Marsh was buryd at Wigan.
-29. dyed a child of Henry Chadockes wife begotten basely by younge Slynhead and poore Henry was cuckolded.

June 1673.

-25. Wednesday night dyed a child of William Apston.
-26. a child of young John Leylands dyed. this evening dyed the wife of Rogr Hasleden cald Shortarme was buryd on the 27 being Friday att Winwicke.

July 1673.

-21. Munday. was buryd att Chappell a child of Ralph Ferehurst.
-23. Wednesday. dyed a child of Nicholas Crowkes.

August 1673.

-1. Friday in the morneing dyed a child from Tho Ralphes who was basely begotten of Elizabeth Leyland de Hadocke p Tho Barrow.
31. lords day. dyed Wiliam Harvie cald Nuttoo he livd with Dr. Sherlocke att Winwicke but came to Ashton and there dyed he was basely conceivd of the body of Ellin Harvie uxor to Roger Lowe senr. and begotten by one Marsh.

September 1673.

-1. Munday A poor woman had a child dyed from John Chadockes in the Flowr Lane and buryed it at Chappell and had none to accompanie her to the funerall but God and herselfe.

   att the same time dyed old Margarie Woorton. She was mother to Dicke that is Esquires Gerards huntsman.

October 1673.

-15. Wednesday. dyed a child of Tho Houghtons was interrd att Chappell.
-18. Saturday ...... was interred two children att Winwicke the one was James and the other Thomas Cloughes being bretheren & sons of old Thomas Clough who was formerly Sr William Gerards huntsman this night about 12 o'clocke dyed old John Robinson was buryd at Chapell.
about this time was buryd a child of Richard Cloughs.
-29. Thursday night. dyed one Tho Hope who some weeks before his death was drinkinge in Joshua Naylors and there had a quarrell with some one who was suposd Joshua gave himm the blow which proved fatell for he nevr lookd up but was upon Friday the 30th. October buryd att Chapell a lustie young chap he was.

November 1673.

-17. Munday. about midnight dyed Margret Orrell widow in the long lane, one that wel spoken of for a good neighbour: was buryd on Wednesday the 19th att Winwicke.
-22. Saturday night. dyed Tho. Bercahll cald king a shoemaker was buryd the othr day at Winwicke.

December 1673.

-14. lords day. dyed half an hower past 12 att noone old Mr. John Saunders att Winwicke.

The Launders of Winwicke, were an old local family, to which there are many enteries referring in the Winwick registers. In the visitation of Lancashire, 1664-5, the marriage of Mr. Arthur Burron, of Warrington, to the daughter of Mr. John Launder, of Winwick, is mentioned.

Jenuery 1673.

-3. Saturday night. dyed a wench of Henry Knowles mason.
-10. lords day. was buryd a still borne child of William Hasleden in town & alsoe the like stil born child of George Low de Lower lane.
-14. thursday. A wench of Thomas Harts.

February 1673.

-14. Saturday. was buryd a lad of Tho Benchalls of the nere Heyes.

99

March 1673-4.

-7. lords day. 2 children of younge Rogr Lowes a twindle.
-11. Wednesday. a child of one Cowlys.
-16. Munday. dyed John Naylor son of Humphrey Naylor the same day a child of Rogr Lowes a twindle about the same time was buryd a child sill borne of Gilbert Cookson was brought in a baskett.
-30. Munday. dyed uxor James Low de Lower Lane.
-31. Tusday. dyed Emme Darbishaire uxor John Darbishire she was my Ems midwife of little Jack a very courteous good woman & her death was much lamented by Em & me.

Aprill 1674.

-i. Wednsday. dyed uxor of Matthew Low her name was Margrett & she was sister to old Em and as Em was goeing towardes her grave Honest Humphrey Harison was sent for backe againe & as it after proved it was to the death of his sister.
-3d. friday. she was buryd & Humphrey occasiond her to be set downe before his feld gate and there was a dolefull and lamentable pteing soe as did effect most that ware present.
        this day dyed sudenslie Ralph Croft son to Lawrance.
-12. Aprill. about one a clock died Joshua Naylor.
-18. Saturday. was buryed att Wiggan Robert Nelson.
-19. lords day. was buryd widow Dusworth daughtr she was maryd towards Lostocke and dyed a childbed.
The whole is 39.

May 1674.

-5. Tusday. dyed old John Marsh very aged & blind.
-6. Wednsday night. dyed old William Darbishire a naylour.
-7. Thursday. there came a lad to the coale pitt with a horse for coales & in looking into the Ginn pitt fell downe and soe was killd, it was not the gin pit, he was sonn to Tho Arowsmith of Lowton Comon.
-24. lords day. was buryd att Chapell old John Lythgoe wife of Westleigh and was mother to John Leyland his wife came to tent her daughter lyeinge in and here dyed.
-29. ffriday. was buryed a twindle of John Leylands.
-30. Saturday. Tho. Calland and wife fled for debt to Ireland and the towne to asist that speedie expedition gave them one fifteene and when they came to Livrple this morneinge theire youngest child dyed and like an hower after its death was buryed and they forthwith tooke shippinge after.
31. lords day. was buryd the other twindle of John Leylands.

June 1674.

-3. Wedensday. was buryd a bastard child of John Hasleden cald fist (?) begotten of one of Throps daughtrs.
-21. lords day. was interred at Chapell a daughtr of William Gerards.
-30. Tusday. dyed Tho. Greenhogh son of John Greenhogh in the Park lane: a lustie fresh young man.
-13. Munday. was interred a litle child of John Hursts.

August 1674.

-7. ffriday night. being or wakes a child of John Turtons.
-8. Saturday. in the afternoone Elizabeth Hey daughtr to Tho Hey de Lilly lane in the pitt in the backeside of the house was drownd.

-12. Wednesday. was interred at Chapell Crofts Cubb an old woman soe cald for her right name I know not.
-29. Saturday. was interred a child new borne of John Ralphson who lived an howr & a half after birth & then dyed.

September 1674.

-5. Saturday. was interred a boy of John Leylands death tooke hime in his foote he was buryd att Chapell.
-7. Munday. dyed William Koxe he was a collier and a very honest man.
-26. Saturday. dyed Anne Kerrison of the towne heath and who had many wintrs there habitated her onely selfe & was very frequent in her discourses with her Cattel as beasts doggs and catts.
-29. tusday. dyed George Kellitt he was Aprentice to Thomas Whittell on Edge Greene.

October 1674.

-10. Saturday. was interred Ann Davies sister to old Litler wife.

Novembr 1674.

-1. Lords day. dyed Ellin Coupe and gave all her goods to John Hunt Gardener att Garswood, all short of expectations.
-14. Saturday. dyed Nicholas Croft a webster yt workedwith Tho Whittle and was buryed this eveninge.

-25. tusday. was interred a child of John Lowes cald Frime it was his eldest daughter.

December 1674.

-6. Lords day. dyed old Jane Whittell mother to Thomas Whitle de Edge Greene its reported that the Spode playeinge upon Edge Greene she had amind to sit in a cheire to heare hime play and Eles Shawe dance not mant weeks before her death and she was 84 yeares of age, and upwards.

Jenuery 1674-5.

-6. Wedensday. being twelth day in Christmas dyed the wife of Rogr Hasleden in the Parke Lane.
-7. Thursday. dyed a child of Tho Summes was buryd att Chapell.
-13. Tusday. dyed a child of John Lowes cald Frime.
-22. Tusday. dyed Rachall Lyon at Bispham Hall who was the housekeaper there and it was reported yt she left Mr. Bispham all shee had wo was 120 li. a very proud young woman she was as I myselfe can witness for being in Holland church one Lords day att the funerall of Samll Darbishires wife I sate in the Peawe with her she could not sit without derision of a poor old man yt sate with us & laught so hartilie as I judgd little devotion in her.
-24. Lords day. dyed a man yt lived on Houghton Hillocke cald Bitter Foote a Strip Hedge an arrant theefe and had sometimes been stockd and was suposd walkd up and down doing acts of theeverie especially striping Hedges and would have come to his son in lawes Dicke a Berchall and there have drunken away his reason in six peny flaggon of those stolne goods and so hopd Mall Dixon round he came to be buryd as they ware takeing Rachell Lyon fro the horse littr bottom to the Beere.
    on this same day was drownd in the Bryn dame a lad of ... Kitts, there was Robert Naylour and one Walkden and this lad noted all three for wicked lads and went into an old Boote that there remained since James Abram was there drownd upon a Lords day too, and as was supposd the Gogleinge of the Boate put them in feare soe much yt the two lads lept out and the boate being overwhelemed, he strechd out his hand for assistance cryd help to this Robert Naylour, who is son to Henry Naylor in the Long lane but hewas not able to pull him out he sunke and was not found till tusday in the afternoone.

Feb 1674-5.

-6. Satturday. we had newes p Preston post that Thomas Rosbottom eldest sonn to Elizabeth Kenion was drowned att Wyre watr and he had been in Ireland certaine yeares and was now come home because imployment faild and stayd with his mother some monthes and wanted a place att last he was prffered to Daniell Chadocke in

102

Preston and was occupied in his service as in rideing about for the prferment of his sale in wines. att this prfam he was occupied in getting wines to shore at Wyre or in seeing it arrived but he was drowned and 3 more he swam the longest of them all & was buryd att Pooton.

-9. Tusday. was buryd a child that dyed from Roge Lowes junr a poor orphan and the constable being John Clough chargd people to goe to ye funerall it was covered in some poor linen but it was brought to the grave without any covering as a very ghostly sight it was suposd to be borne in or about Standish.

-26. Friday. was buryd old Rogr Hasleden cald short arme.

-27. Saturday. was buryed old Peter Berchalls wife of Edge green.

March 1674.

-6. Saturday. dyed Tho Ashton out of Long-lane.

-23. tusday. was buryed att Winwicke Tho. Lyon a young man owned Crumbery Lee in the Parke lane and was involved in such debts as his Land was suposd would not redeem and had nothing to live on but what his sister Eles in Cheshire where he dyd from did releeve he was very unfortunate in his life.

-24. Wednesday. dyed a child of Tho. Whitles de Edge-greene.

-31. tusday. dyed a child of John Callands Blackesmith.

Aprill 1675.

-3. Saturday. dyed a child of Raph Cunley collier.

-21. Wedensday. was interred at Chapell William the son of Gilbert Cookeson.

-28. Wedensday. was buryd att Chapell a child of William Tahlore Collier. 42 in all.

May 1675.

-i. Saturday. came through the Towne Willia Bradshaw borne in Neawten and dyd at Brimscald - death and was to be he dyd att his fathrs house in Neawton and so buryd att Winwicke.

-20. Thursday. Cozen Robert Rosbothom had his Benjamin the youngest taken from hime by the fatefull hand of death aged about 15 monthes.

-29. Saturday. dyed uxor John Houghton Bawbally.

June 1675.

-6. Lords day. in the morneinge about sun riseinge dyed Mary Knowles Tho. Knowles barley man and and his eldest sister whose death was much bewailed a very hopeful younge woman and is now without question arived att her wished haven of rest she writt down with her one hand the text to be preached att her funerall which was 120 ps. 5 wo is me yt sojourne in Mesech the consideration of which makes her the more bewailed now dead she forethought her death in the time of her health and is now in blisse.

-7. Munday. dyed Robert Leyland Blackesmith.

-9. Wedensday. was buryd att Chapell a child of widow Hopes.

-16. Wedensday. about half an hour past 2 of the clock this afternoone dyed old Olliver Potter he was a shoomaker by trade very dilligent in his callinge, a constant keaper of his shop no sooner had old age rendrd him useless in his shop but he tooke it so to hart as never looked up after it.

-23. Wedensday. dyed Mr. James Sorowcold of Eyebridge.

-24. Thursday. dyed Richard Talbott de Parke lane.

-25. Friday. dyed Alexander Potter 3d. son to Cozen John Potter de Lilly Lane who in his life time was nevr supposd to have any genius a meer child yet now att his death cald father & mother & prayd forgivenes of his faults in cheating them of a half peny and wished them to live in peace & that his sister Ellin would leave off swearinge & so dyed & without question is now att rest.

July 1675.

-11. Lords day. dyed old Humphrey Naylor de Parke lane.

        this same Lords day Edwrad Dusworth his sonne was drownd in a pitt with batheinge his name was Jack.

-27. Tusday night. dyed James Hasleden de Gladdin Hey Browe Locksmith he was very defformed in bodie like Beanesheafe.

August 1675.

-15.Lords day. dyed a famale child & the first borne of Thomas Harrison Skinner.

-18. Wedensday. abut 10 of the clocke dyed Mr. Coe att Eye bridge he was schoole Mr. there to Mr. Sorowcold's child & one yt Mr. Sorowcold's child & one yt Mr. Sorowcold reposd great trust in the Tutoringe of his sonne & left him 10li. p annum & his diet till his sonnes came of age phisicke not workinge till after death made him wysre (?)

-about the 4th of August dyed a chamber maid from Garswood.

-25. Wedensday. dyed Elles or Margret Tickle she was housekeeper att eye bridge & so left p Mr. Sorowcold 7 there dyed this is the 3d yt is dead fro thence in a few weekes all dyed in a hot feaver.

-30. about 1 a clocke in the night diyed uxor Tho. Clough.

-31. Tusday. dyed Jame Harvie one who too earlie in her prime of her yeares assented to lust Temptations by committing ffornication with Raph Johnson by whom she had 3 or 4 children 7 was never maryed to hime being ore come by his too eager solicitations which provd the impoverishment of her selfe and parents yet notwithstanding she kept sole from any other & onely livd to cary the badge of Raph Jenkins Concubin yt her Laudablence & so the reproech justilie redounds to Raph the too Luxurious Luster.

Sept 1675.

-12. Lords day. dyed Izibell Whittell sister to Tho. Whittell a mallencholly women allwayes att seldom or never seene adroad either att church or markett.
-17. Fryday. was interred a child of the Millrs of the Bryn.
-26. Lords day. dyed Ellen uxr James Worthington.

October 1675.

-5. Tusday. about 2 of the clocke this afternoone dyed Mr. Cuthbert Clifton the great & profane monster of Jesuiticall impietie his abode was and had beene longe att Brynne & Garswood where he dyed.
-16. Saturday. dyed Mary Harper in Longlane daughter to James Harper.
-19. Tusday. on Wiggin Fair day dyed Henry Kenion of ye hole he hath an estate in Lower lane.

Novembr 1675.

- Elezebeth Naylor mothr to Tho Naylor de Gladdin Hey dyed this day.
-22. Tusday. was interred att Chapell old Gabriall wife of a poor woman yt had rec 4s. p month out of Town leige (? leye).

Decembr 1675.

-7. Tusday. dyed Katherin the wife of James Hasleden Locksmith de Senellie Greene who dyed unpectedlie & sudeinlie tho' old yet well and dead in one day.
-16. Thursday. dyed old Tho. Leech of the Coalpitts.
-29. Wedensday night. dyed James Darbishire who was brought & lived a protestant & had maryed Dicke Ashtone widow oditer of Louds Coal pitt who was a papist till now she maryed hime all the while he was a husband he was as I may say Metemorphosed to wt he was before it pleased god to visit hime with sickenes & then she turnd her religion & was a meanes in his languishment to turne him which he did and so dyed.

A very sad story if rightly undrstood for young men to be careful both whom and where they marry.
[Note here. - John Leyland His book, 1728.]

Jannery 1675.

-3. Munday. dyed Richard Marsh he worked with cozen Robert at ye Whitesmiths trade.

-6. Thursday night. about 6 of the clocke dyed John Darbishire father to the afforesaid James who expressd before his death yt sons being perverted by papits had burst his hart.

-21. Ffriday night. about 6 a clocke a lad of Rogr Naylors maltman dyed.

Febuery 1675.

-4. Friday. Newes was brought to this Town p Henry Pearsies man that Thomas Jenkins second sonne to John Jenkins Landed man was dead att Sturbridge who was envited thither p his Elder brother which brothr thither for fornication.

-6. Lords day. Margrett the wife of David Pendleberie de Lowbanke was delivrd of two Twindles and the one dyed and was buryd att Chappell.

About 17 or 17th day dyed a child of Henry Wrights.

March 1675.

-3. Friday. about 5 a clocke in the morneinge dyed that mirour of providence & house keaper Eles wife of Peter Leyland.

Also about the same time depted that monster of extravagancie & gluttone Margret Greenhogh this day notice is given that young Slynehead who had committed folly with Chadockes wife de Sendaly green in Chadocks absence was dead at Sturbridge.

-6. Munday morneinge. dyed uxor of Henry Wright de Long lane.

And old Katherin Edleston mother to Laurance de Cro.... she was well on Saturday.

-10. Friday. dyed a girle of Mathew Chadocke in ye Towne.

-28. Tuesday. in Easter week dyed Henry Hurt (civill to all men) if any thing intemperate or imodestly was as to the first to himselfe as to the 2dy in his superfluous talke, but ever of a generous dispodition & of the vulge wel beloved my lad John went to his funerall his Unkle Tho Harison carry hims to the bells & up Steeple & the night after he dreamed of a Long Steeple this was the first time he was att Winwick or att a buryall.

April 1676.

-8. Saturday. Mr. Peter Bradshaw the popish priest at Brynne Hall was this day interred att Wiggan he was Unkle to sr. Rogr. Bradshaw of Hay.

-12. Wedensday. was maryed James Low to Katherin Seddon of Ince.

-18. Tuesday. slept in Jesus that incomperable practitioner of Christiantie Coz Robert Rosbotham who livd desird of all and dyed lamented of all very useful in this place a

loveing & dear husband a tender harted father a right good neighbour and a very pious
Christian one who livd justly t his neighbour soberlie to himself piously to god so yt if
a man would take Compendium or delver it upon sacred scripture to show which a
one a christian ought to be (this onely unpeleld mans life was or held out the whole
volume of scared writ) the like pelell I do not know in all ye world a first tablle & a
second table Christian not one in profession & another in conversation but as was his
pfession so was his practice holy just and gracious in all his proceedings so yt if a man
would to the life studie wt a one a christian ought to be in a Gospell sence he needed
not to repair scarcely any where els but to the life of this eminant Saint this holy man
St. Robert now departd but the onely wise god thgought the earth not wothie such a
jewill should longe sojourne here & as if the Serephims & blessed Saints above ware
restless till the holy man were invested with themselves in glory on purpose to make
their heavenlie mellodi more harmonious the same god calld hime to his rest to the
pticipation ofhis heavenly joyes about two of the clocke this same Tuesday which day
he had cald gods people together for humiliation & yt god appointed for his day of
exaltation his fight being fought his warefare accomplished beacsuse he had kept the
faith and now hath received the crowne att his age of 46 he had in devibe things the
Serpents wisdom with the sweet mixture of the doves inocence he was a right
Abraham in his household government & amidst diffidences a right Joshua for
courage & for uprightness & faith a very David whose faith was builded an the
promises a sincere Hezekiah and inded a true hearted Nathaniall in whom was no
guile & for that christian grace of selfe denyall his ordenerie course & practice was
rather to injure himeselfe then comitt a sin or lye to get gaine as proved in those suites
he had with Rothwell tho' the Lord helped him out of all & gave such a testimonie of
his likeing yt he prosperd in all his desires.

[Since 1 May 1675 to May 1676 dyed 44.]

May 1676.

-3. Wedensday. was interred att Chapell a poor womans child.
-7. Munday. dyed old Litler wife de Senally green.
-16. Whitsunday tusday. dyed Nicholas Houghton's wife.
-18. Thursday. dyed John Lowe de Dame End.
-19. Ffriday. a son of Edward Houghtons.
-22. Munday. was interred att Standish Mr. John Bowth my Loveing friend a very fat
man he had been at Deanes Court & gott att Chorley & gott a fall which proved his
death.
-24. Notice was come yt Barkr yt maried Peg Widows was dead in Ireland - not dead.
-28. lords day. was interred uxr Will Withington de Parke Lane.

June 1676.

-9. Friday. this morninge dyed Margret Winterbothom and Thomas Knowles Barleyman. I went with hime about Februery into Cople beyond Standish to view a younge woman and staying over late and comeinge home in the night we saw in the field next beyond Brynn damme an Aperition he saw it first & then I in likeness to a coffin upright and moveing at first towards us then froward us in the same way we went and att bridge went down & vanishd but we were both frightened.
-17. Saturday. The Shawe one yt worked in Mr. Jamesons marle pitt was well & dead in one hours time it is suposd he was sweletd.
-20. Tusday. a child new borne of Tho. Foxes.
-28. Tuesday. dyed uxr John Hasleden de Gladin Hey.
-29. Wedensday. dyed uxr Lawrance croft de Towne.

July 1676.

-12. Wedensday. about noone dyed old Tho. Lee de Whitleighe green nevr maried.
-29. Wedensday. dyed James Harrys a young man.
-18. Tusday ..... Tho. Berchall had one eye was speechless a weeke.
-20. Thursday. a child of Esqr. Gerard.

August 1676.

-1. Munday night. dyed Emme Lowe de Senallie Greene a fresh lustie young woman.
-2. Tusday. this morninge was found dead in bed old Cardman als Richardson the two releeved hime, a nastie tho a fad specticle to behold dureinge his weaknes.

September 1676.

-28. Thursday. was interred a younge borne child of Henry Harte.

October 1676.

-24 Tuesday. was interred the wife of John Strange formerlie the wife of David Pendleberie whitesmith.
-30 h. Munday. dyed Nicholas Cronke of Edg green.

November 1676.

-2. Thursday. being our Court day was buryed one Bett Morriss.

-6. Munday. dyed that Sicophant Edward Stockley whose pillicie and naturall indowments tended to the subversion of the poore Tenants being Stewerd att Garswood & is now dead & hath receivd the reward of his deserts like a disembling knave as he was.

-20. Munday night. between the hours of 12 and 1 of the clocke depted this life Madam Gerard Esq Gerards wife who was sister to Sr. Tho. Preston a very charitable women.

-26. Lords day. Elizabet Pendleberie mother to David went on this day to enquire after a brother in Bishinge was conceivd to be concerned in drinke came late to Thomas Simes and by reason of the darkness of the night and most through advise of Dicke Pemberton went to Tho. Hasledon's who livd on Senenllie greene & yt barbarous base women refusd to rise to let her in & soe she made homewards and between Tho. Stanges and Tho. Leeches in lane went into a ditch a deepe one and was sudlin dubled and with founderinge to get the skin of her armes was ..... of & there remained till 4 a clocke the other morneinge and 2 lads coming to their worke found her state a copp betwixt Tho. Leeches & ye lane yt leads to John Clarkes house upon information thereof to Lawrance Pendleberie who got assistanle & brought her home & in half an hower after shee came to ye fire she dyed an excellent woman for hospitalite.

-29. Wedensday. was interred a daughtr of Robert Greenoughs who was dead & well att an instant.

December 1676.

-1. Friday. a daughtr of William Darbishires.

-7. Thursday. dyed uxr John Greenough de Parke lane.

-24. John enkinson Landed man came fro Sturbridge and brought the newes of younge Swinehead who was interred thursday seavenight before.

-27. wedensday. dyed Dammeris Naylour.

Januerie 1676.

-13. Saturday night. James the eldest sonne of Lawrance Edleston dyed of a paine in his knee it was suposed to be the evill a very courteous and hopefull young man & without contriversie is now in heaven.

-23. Thursday. was brought to bed John Shawes wife & had a wench still borne.

-att this time a child of John Wooten..

-12. Munday. was dead William the first borne of James Lowe de Towne about 4 days old.

-25. Thursday. was interred att Chappell Susan the wife of Robert Tailour.

Ffeb. 1676.

-8 Thursday. about the howers of 9 & 10 of the clocke in the eveninge dyed Elin Rigbie one who had been in great extrenitie a good while and had lived to se the death of her husband and children she was sadly efflicted with the evil in so much as Tho Harioson her elbow bone tooke out, being rot from the rest.-26. Munday. dyed Raph Lowe Dams end an honest poor man.

March 1676.

-5. Munday. this morneinge wasa found dead Ellin Lowe of the Towne green a harmless quiet neighbour.
-7. Wedensday. was buryd old Dill a Lealand & Beadlomes sonns child had by Morris daughtr.
-18. Lords day. dyed prateling John Fletcher de Lowr lane he was observd to be a very proud man both in gate and aparral and one yt gloryed in his one discourse.

Aprill 1677.

-6. ffriday. was interred Joseph the sonn of Jefferie Berchall he was leprous about 2 years of age and he grew from te middle upward had a head a bigge as 3.
-16. Munday. was interred a child of James Byroms.
-20. Ffriday. dyed my good friend Peter Low de Edge Greene and also a child of Devid Pendleberies this eveninge dyed an old woman cald Meggie Calland. all these ware buryed on Saturday the first being Peter Low, haveing a colt that had beene cutt & with farcie & cutting was soe lowe as was not able to goe out of the house and yet the night before its death got out of the houseinge and walked up & downe in the Lane it selfe [they] conceived this to be an omen or a prsage of Peters death as it behoved afterwards and the death of the colt was some trouble to Peter on his death bed.
-21. Saturday. dyed Devid Pendleberie a litle before sunsettinge when we ware home from his childes funerall it was suposd that drinkeing hurt hime.
-25. ffriday. dyed Tho. Gerard de Hollin Hey on the Munday before he was on horsebacke in tendinge to the funerall of Devid Pendleberie but sickness at yt jucture surprised hime and he was constarind to retreate he was a man of a sober temperate and very solid judicious nature and a very usefull man in the effaires of the towne all his failance yt ever I could discerne was he was a litle too curious in prieing too high above the starrs of an astronomicall nature fforetellinge future events but in the close of his dayes I thinke he was much reformed and I thinke he was a good man tho he did busie himselfe too much in the planytane orbe and starie constallation but whiles he kept amongst us in this world out of the planats below the torrid zone he was a good neighbour and would have arged very well just in his dealeings and in all respects very well accomplished with good morrall pts - in all 48.

May 1677.

-26. Saturday. Mrs. Jane Lanckton dyed was well at 6 o'clock in the eveninge & dead .... she was sadlie possessed of Satan in a corporall sense as it was expresst yt Satan would speake to her & shee to hime.

-28. Munday. was interred Rogr Lowe junior de Penybrooke.

June 1677.

-6. thursday. Ellin the widow of Tho Kighley came to live in ye house where James Lanckton dyd out of and ye day after shee came she dyd they livd 7 dyd on Edge green att Crocks.

-16. Saturday dyed Ellin uxr Bawin Atherton and on this day was buryd Mrs. Mosse mothr.

July 1677

- Ffriday. about day dyed John Ashton of thee Crosse he lived and dyed fro Ralph Hasledens housd of the Dock lane left 7 children behind hime ane from his one estate was newlie elected evrseer of the highway and in yt office dyed he was a meeke quiet naturde man & a good neighbour.

-14. Saturday. was interred 2 new borne twindles of James Chadockes of Whiteleighe greene.

-28. Peter Harte.

August 1677.

-1. Wedensday. was interred Thomas Leyland Roberts sonn.

-17. ffriday. a little wench of Raph Ferehurst.

September 1677.

-1. Saturday. a child of Richard Berchalls yt.

-12. Wedensday. was well & dead att an instant Peter Aspinall.

-21. a child of Henry Raphenson was interred att chappell.

October 1677.

-19. ffriday a sill borne child of John Rapheson.

111

-23. tusady. a child of John Goodings. this same day before 6 of the clocke in ye eveninge departed Robert Naylor of the Long lane who hath remained in a languishing state as in the conceivd ever since litle kitts drowneing in the milldamme he being in the companie.

-24. Wedensday night. dyed William Hasleden junr whose greatest fault was to be too observant of his fathrs commandments [which] ware two (i) doe noe good, doe mot communtcate thy goods to beggrs [the] world if full [of them] and the (2) was; trust thee noe bodie, lending nothing, all the world is knaves, and by this may be guessed what a oseless man he was att his age eyther to the neighbour or to the poore, a men yt livd secure, would neithr borrow nor lend, nor in noe respect upon noe ecct would accomodate any neighbour with the least good, however necessity for any an in his generall conversation to conceite the world patcht up of nithing but begers and knaves in a great peece pollicie to retaine what amand hath but a disgrace to Christanitie for as the former keapes hime fro chartie so the other keapes hime in distrust not to doe good or to be a publicke instrument for good in the place he lives in when the necessitie of ones neighbour calls for it denotes a men worser in some feases then heathens.

-31. Wedensday dyed old William Hasleden he ridd to Winwicke ffriday before to his sons interment wordly minded caitiff he was in all   coneerness as may prove suffciuntlie by the former relacion.

November 1677.

-13. Munday. dyed a litle child of Henry Lowes de Low banke.
-22. thursday. dyed Eles the second wife to Bryan Sixsmith she was sister to Hmphrey Carter a carefull industrious woman.

December 1677.

-8. Saturday. was interred Jeffrie Cookeson idiott.
-15. Saturday. dyed Mary uxr James leyland she was sister to John Pendleberie.
-20. Thursday. dyed old Edward Clarke collier de Lower Lane and old professor.
-24. Munday night. dyed Henry Bercall cald Noser Hary.
-27. Thursday. dyed old Bryan Lowe de Lower Lane.
-27. dyed a sonne of Lawrance Edleston de Crosse.
-31. Munday. dyed the onely daughtr & child of Ellin Lowe widow de Rummers field.

Januery 1677.

-16. Wedensday. dyed John Houghton about noone a most sad terible swearer & drinker & the same day dyed Ellin Calland.

-26. Saturday. was interred Mr. Farington a priest at Brynn yt there had lived 16 years and was the housekeaper there or caterer for the priest.

Feb. 1677.

-i. Ffriday. dyed Eles Lyon matyed to John Ashbroke in Hellsbie in Cheshire and from thence brought to Winwicke and there interred dyed of an impost.
-4. Munday. dyed uxr Peter Williams from Edg Greene.

March 1677.

-1. ffriday. dyed John Rosbothom de Crosse whitesmith.
-9. Saturday. was interred Robert Laylands widow.
-12. Tusday. dyed Eles Harvie had a cancer in her breast she lived with old Dr. Cloughs widow.
-15. ffriday. dyed Mary Lashley a servant att Garswood.

Aprill 1678.

-17. Wedensday. was interred a child of Henry Hodgson.
in all 38.

May 1678.

-15. Lords day. dyed uxor of William Crumpton in childbed she was Robert Worthingtons daughtr.
-10. ffriday. dyed John Jaxon eldest sonn to Tho Jaxon who had been a considerable time lame and was very impotent.

August 1678.

-i. Thursday. dyed William Woorston shoomaker he was old Dr. Woorston brother an honest poor man.
-27. Tusday. dyed Elizebeth Knowles 8 felton wife.

September 1678.

-1. Lords day night. dyed Rogr Hasleden de Parke Lane yeom.

-19. ffriday. about 10 a clock in the afternoon dyed old Thomas Winstanley of the Town Yate.
-29. Lords day. was interred a child of Joseph Gerard.

October 1678.

-2. Wedensday night. dyed Eles uxr John Smith.
-15. Tusday. a child of Joseph Knowles.

Novembr 1678.

-2. Saturday. was interred a child of Georg Durdoms.
-5. Tusday. dyed a child of John Cronkes.
-11. Munday dyed John Chadockes son of Witt Chadocke Whitleigh green.
-14. Thursday. Edward Marsh went to the funerall of old John Orford de Haydocke & his child was drowned in hole.
-24. Lords day. a child of Raph Fewhursts.

December 1678.

-30. Lords day. a boy of Lawrance Sedon dyed through his mothers tableing in another house and leaving her children in her house was sadly burnt to death.

> The last portion of the obituary is a mere record of burials from 1661 to 1669 at which Roger Lowe was present. The list is interesting from the many local names and references. On the last page of the book in which the diary is written is a list of kings of the Saxon Heptarchy evidently written out by the diarist.

-2. October 1660. Henry Boendman dyed Nells son a child.
-14. October 1660. John Jenkinson son of Mathew buryed at Ffarnworth.
-21. February 1660. was interred at St. Ellins Josiah Churle.
-24. March 1660. dyed young Georg Bradshaw clarke of Leigh.
-3. July 1661. dyed Mr. Charnley Ashton schoolemaster.
-2. August 1661. dued William Byrom of Downell greene.
-30. December 1661. dyed dr. Richard Gerard.
-21. Feb 1661. friday night dyed William Craine.
-14. March 1661. ffriday about Cockes Crow or before dyed Gawther Tailour.
-10. Aprill Thursday 1662. was interred James Jolley had beene a courtier.
-1662 12 Aprill. was interred old Dr. Clough.
-31. May 1662. Paule Houghton falling from his harle (?) eart in Docke Lane broke his necke.

-1662. June 12. Tho the eldest sonne of Ralph Hasleden dyed at Hughes Hindley in Westleigh of the Pockes.

-19. June 1662. dyed Ann daughtr of Hugh Hindley of the Pockes.

-23. was buryed Bryan Lowes last wife. June 1662.

-1. July 1652 dyed Elizabeth Higginson shee was sister to Rogr Naylor Glasier.

-25. July 1662 was buryed John Pendleberie eldest of Robert Penbleberie.

-5. November 1662 Peter Burscee.

-8. November. was buryed old John Madocke de Crowe Lane and Tho. Burscoe they both being pius folkes mett att the ffurther end of Neawton and went to the church togethr.

-2. Januery 1662. dyed William Stanly from Bryan Lowes & left his Estate to emme uxr Peter Aspinwall: William Marsh dyd Whitleigh greene.

-5. Feb, 1662. John Chadocke fellow Apprentice was maryd.

-17. March 1662. dyed Margrett Hill daughtr to Ellin uxr Mathew Raphes.

-14. May 1663. Edward Calland of crosse was buryd.

-4. June 1663 old Rich Mrs. Duckenfield of Bickerstaffe was buryd she was aged.

-1. August 1663. Saturday was interred old John Tankerfeild att Winwicke.

-29. August 1663. dyed Eles Leyland Jauvis sister a good woman.

-7. September. munday 1663. Hamblett Ashton was hanged at Chester for killing a Tapster in Nantwich in Cheshire.

-3. Januery 1663. old James Haryes went out of the house being a darke night & plunged into the pitt & was drowned he lived att James Berchalls near Jeand barne.

-14. June 1664. a daughtr of Raph Hasleden very young of the Docke Lane was a suddeinly dead her mothr had laid rotten meat for mice & the Girle had receivd it through her mothrs carlesness in laying it.

-11. July 1664. was buryd Tho. Tailor de Sankey he was Gawthurs Tailor brother.

-22. August 1664. Lucie the wife of the afforesaid named Thomas Tailor was buryed they ware both buryd on a sunnday & left greate Riches no man knew how.

-10. September 1664. was buryd old Asmull of Seneley Greene Dickes father.

-16. September 1664. dyed Richard Bordman.

-2. October 1664. was buryed old John Jenkins the flowr of that generation.

-13. December 1664. was buryd Henry theeldest sonn of Willm Ashton de Whitleigh Green.

-2. Januery 1664. was buryed Jane Pottr Coz Johns daughtr.

-9. Januery 1664. my brothr Williams son cald Raph was buryd att St. Ellines Chappell.

-7. Februery 1664. Tusday. was buryed Jospeh Naylor de Edgge Greene.

-9. Februery. 1664. Thursday. was buryd Mr. Thomas Blackebourne of Blackly Hurst.

-3. Aprill 1665. Mr. Henry Banister was drawen on a Litter dead through this Towne being slain by Colket att Sr Philip Edgrton att a Race on Forrest of Da la Mare.

-3. Aprill 1665. dyed Ann Johnson Tho Jenkins wives sister was buryd att Standish.

-11. Aprill 1665. was interred Grace Gerard at Manchester a young women unmarried.

-31. June 1665. was interred Mrs. Mary Rosthorne mother to Mr. Atherton of Atherton and Beawsey.

-14. August 1665. was interred a female child of Joshua Naylors.

-19. January 1665. was interred old Mrs. Birch her husband was a reader & schoole Mr. att Ashton.

-5. ffebruary 1665. dyed my sister Elin in childbed.

-25 March 1666. was interred old Allin's wife George Allines mother.

-30 March 1666. a son of Raph Low of the Dane end in Downell Greene was apprentice with John Clough came from his Mr. house to his Fathers and hanged himself.

-8. June 1666. was buryd Margret uxr old John Jenkinson she was cald old Cocke.

-13. October 1666. old Mr. Bankes of Winstanley was interrd.

-15. December 1666. was interred Mr. John Blakeburne.

-16. December 1666. was interred Anne Taylor Aunt Pegges daughter.

-21. December 1666. dyed Elizabeth uxr old Will Hasleden.

-2. Januery 1666. was interred Coz John Pottrs eldest son named John a very hopefull youth.

-21. february 1666. Lords day. night dyed old Mr. James Woodes.

-20. July 1667. was interred Thomas Leech of the Towne Inkeaper.

-8. Septembr 1667. Munday. was buryd mr. Pottr formerlie Margret Lyons uxor Rich Lyon Parke Lane.

-13. Januery 1668. was interred at Gropnall in Cheshire Mrs. Woods with her husband.

25. Feb. 1668. was buryd Richard Landers Mr. Landrs brothr he dyed out of Hoome.

-19. March. 1668. was interred the daughtr of Tho. Potter named Margrett.

       Two leaves backward are the names of such as dyd within my Aprntiship and providentialle I was calld to the funeral.